CLASSIC BUS

YEARBOOK – 6

CW00349084

EDITED BY GAVIN BOOTH

Ian Allan
PUBLISHING

CONTENTS

First published 2000

ISBN 0 7110 2749 8

Design by Hieroglyph

Published by Ian Allan Publishing

an imprint of Ian Allan Publishing Ltd, Terminal House, Station Approach, Shepperton, Surrey TW17 8AS
Printed by Ian Allan Printing Ltd, Riverdene Business Park, Molesey Road, Hersham, Surrey KT12 4RG

Code: 0005/B1

INTRODUCTION

Every two months *Classic Bus* magazine offers readers the best articles and stories about buses the way they used to be. And for the past six years, there has been the bonus of a *Yearbook* to allow a further wallow in nostalgia.

This sixth *Yearbook* covers motorbuses and trolleybuses over the last 70 or 80 years, with particular emphasis on the postwar years that an increasing number of *CB* readers remember.

From the early days of motorbus operation there is Alan Oxley's article on that fascinating transport pioneer, T. H. Barton, and the advertisements and vehicles of the 1930s are recalled in 'The way we were'.

Philip Mountford looks back at the buses he remembers in North Staffordshire in the 1930s and 1940s, and Ted Shepherd describes life as a London bus conductor working out of Athol Street in the late 1940s and early 1950s.

The 'Bonny Buses', mid-1950s double-deckers, are fondly described by David Wayman, and Malcolm Flynn utters the words of so many enthusiasts recalling missed opportunities – 'If only I'd . . .'.

The products of Britain's major coachbuilders are well known to *CB* readers, but there were always smaller companies with regular and faithful customers. Martyn Nutland tells the story of Heaver. And Geoff Burrows looks at the Bedford SB, at one time one of the most familiar chassis on British roads.

The trolleybus had only a brief lifespan in the UK, peaking after the 1930s boom, and disappearing from our streets by the early 1970s. Michael Dryhurst writes about the final years of Britain's trolleybuses, which he visited courtesy of the Co-operative movement!

Coming more up to date, there is a feature on Scotland in 1975, the year regionalisation was introduced, Hugh Dougherty looks at CIE's E class Leyland Leopards in Donegal, and Peter Haines pays tribute to Southend's 33ft long Daimler Fleetlines. There has been a long tradition of exporting British double-deckers for tourist and promotional work, and Richard Bellingham looks at the Swiss-based Londag company.

We include some familiar features from *Classic Bus* magazine. Alan Millar has contributed four Checkpoint features, giving instant information on very different subjects; Alan has also nominated another *Wonderbus*, as an antidote to the regular magazine feature, Classic Blunderbus; John Aldridge has written an I Was There piece on how Northern General had the nerve to suggest that the Leyland National could be improved; and Geoff Burrows has cracked the Bristol chassis codes.

Enjoy the sixth *CB Yearbook*. If you haven't discovered the magazine yet, you'll find it in good newsagents and bookstalls.

Gavin Booth
Edinburgh

Front cover: *Capturing a once-familiar scene in the West Midlands, the 1965 ex-Midland Red D9 no.5399 (BHA 399C), now preserved at the BaMMoT museum at Wythall.*
John Robinson

Page 1: *The trolleybus enjoyed a fairly brief, but successful, life in the UK. On page 80 Michael Dryhurst remembers catching up with the remaining systems in their final years. Wolverhampton was one of the largest systems, and Michael's photo shows two Guy BTs of 1949, with Park Royal 54-seat bodies, at the terminal loop in Dudley. Like many municipal operators, Wolverhampton supported local industry; Guy had is factory in the town, as did Sunbeam, which also supplied trolleybuses to Wolverhampton Corporation.*
Michael Dryhurst

Back cover, upper: *Lancashire United is one of Britain's best-remembered independent bus fleets. No.187 (RTC 352C), a Northern Counties-bodied Guy Arab V, is seen at Bolton's Moor Lane bus station in May 1973.*
Ron Robinson

Back cover, lower: *Morecambe & Heysham Corporation no.507 (KTF 586), a 1949 AEC Regent III with Park Royal body, in Heysham Road, Morecambe in August 1973*
Ron Robinson

BONNY BUSES

DAVID WAYMAN considers some contenders for the title

Above: *Representing the 'mature' motor bus of the mid-1950s. Nottingham no.272 (XTO 272), a 1956 AEC Regent V/Park Royal 62-seater, seen in Standhill Road in April 1957.*
Roy Marshall

OH, BUT there were some bonny buses coming into service around 45 years ago. Take those Park Royal-bodied exposed radiator AEC Mk V Regents of Nottingham Corporation, for instance. What lovely-looking vehicles they were! Their proportions were comely. They were pleasing on the eye from various aspects. Everything about them seemed well thought-out. Yes, of course I realise that not everyone will necessarily agree as to what is attractive or otherwise. It comes down to personal taste. Yet I suggest that those Nottingham Regents, numbered 209 to 238 (UTV 209 etc) and 239 to 273 (XTO 239 etc) of 1955 and 1956 were among the best of double-deckers ever built, at least so far as appearance was concerned. Their respective layouts were H33/28R and H34/28R.

They represented the 'mature' motorbus of the middle-1950s. Mechanically, the models of chassis then available were well-built, reliable and generally economical. Other than at the small and less expensive end of the market there was virtually no competitor to the diesel engine. Such units as those produced by AEC, Leyland and Gardner were widely accepted and giving satisfactory service. Improved lubricants and chromium-plated piston rings were enhancing engine life significantly. Bodybuilders had overcome some of the prewar niggles associated with metal-framed bodies. Timber-framed ones had recovered from the difficulties of the 1940s when proper seasoning had not always been practicable. Indeed, bodies and chassis had perhaps become a little too robust. This had resulted in some relatively high unladen weights. In 1939, few double-deckers weighed more than seven tons. By the early 1950s, some of them were considerably more than eight tons, although many of these were 6in wider and 1ft longer than prewar buses. Operators' concerns about running costs had led to a trend toward lighter buses by about 1953. Some 'deckers then had unladen weights nearer to prewar levels. This cut costs on fuel, tyres and some components.

Left: **Other Park Royal bodies produced during the early part of the 1950s incorporated London RT type proportions. The example on 1953 East Kent Guy Arab IV GFN 913 shows the effect of lengthening by 1ft and widening by 6in to 27ft x 8ft dimensions.**
David Wayman

Below: **In Rochdale's distinctive blue/ivory livery, no.254 (KDK 654), a 1954 Daimler CVG6 with a shapely Weymann 59-seat body complementing the Daimler tin front.**
John Fozard

Those Nottingham Regent Vs had the AEC 9.6litre engine, four-speed synchromesh gearbox and vacuum brakes. With an unladen weight of just over $7\frac{1}{4}$ tons the power was ample. The Mk V was usually a lighter chassis than the well-established Mk III which largely owed its origins to a London Transport development of 1938, going into production for provincial customers in 1946/7. Instead of the Mk III's 9.6litre power unit, some Regent Vs had the then newly-introduced AV470 engine which AEC called its 7.75litre unit although in fact the swept volume was 7.685litre. Others had the trusty Gardner 8.4litre 6LW. The Mk V was also offered with the options of the four-speed preselective gearbox (well-proved in the Mk III) and what was then a new form of direct-acting semi-automatic gearbox to which AEC gave the name 'Monocontrol'. Air brakes were an alternative to the vacuum kind in some cases.

Tin front

At that time it was fashionable for double-deckers to have a concealed radiator behind a so-called 'tin front' instead of the conventional exposed radiator shell. The new trend had developed from early postwar efforts by the manufacturer Foden and the operator Midland Red, followed by Birmingham Corporation which used the same design of front on Crossley, Daimler and Guy chassis. The second two of those were marketing their chassis with the tin front by the mid-1950s, Guy also offering the traditional exposed shell for those who preferred it. AEC had its own versions of the 'new look', as it was also called at that time, and it could be argued that the MKV type was the most attractive of them all. Nottingham City Transport, however, chose the optional exposed item complete with the inevitable triangular badge. Few enthusiasts would fail to gain satisfaction from the appearance of the long-accepted and familiar AEC forward-engined chassis front end.

The only way in which it could possibly have been improved on the Mk V was by chromium-plating the radiator shell.

The appearance of bonny-looking chassis could be spoiled by an unattractive body. Nottingham's Regent Vs offered the best of both worlds. Apart from that lovely radiator shell, the chassis' looks were enhanced by the use of rear wheel discs, characteristic front wheel nut rings and delicately-shaped Mk III-type front wings. As to the bodywork, from 1938 (wartime 'utility' period excepted) Park Royal had offered a double-decker with a pleasantly curving frontal rake. This was virtually standard for postwar highbridge production. Then, from 1950, many of Park Royal's metal-framed bodies were built to a four-bay design with London RT-family proportions, some of them widened to 8ft. Of course, Park Royal was the major RT body builder, achieving an output of more than 3,000 during the seven years from 1947. In 1954, this RT-based provincial design was refined. The main windows were altered to about the same depth as those of the Park Royal's five-bay designs as supplied previously to Nottingham, among others. The lower edges of the front bulkhead windows were curved

Above: *In 1955/6 Birkenhead bought exposed radiator Guy Arab IVs with handsome Massey 59-seat bodies, represented here by no.378 (EBG 750) of 1956. The combination of the tough, dependable Guy Arab and the durable, well-built Massey body resulted in an eminently serviceable and trouble-free bus.*
John Fozard

down from the centre, assisting forward visibility for downstairs passengers. The twin windows of the upper saloon emergency exit were curved to match the curvature of the dome, helping to keep the profile smooth. Overall, the effects were cleaner and neater. In Nottingham's case, further enhancement was added by the livery of a medium green with three relieving cream bands and black beading to separate the colours. The wheels were bright red and the wings black. Forward-facing vents at the front of the upper saloon and four sliding vents per side in both saloons provided yet more beautification. For the first time in Nottingham, a 'T'-shaped layout of destination and service number apertures was adopted at front and rear. This was an innovation of fleet engineer Mr F. Thorpe which he took with him later as general manager to Bury and then Newport. The UTV-registered batch were among the earliest buses in the country to have flashing direction indicators, produced locally and positioned in this case on the lower saloon waistrail. Internally, the seats were trimmed with green leathercloth-type covering. The windows were flush with their finishers and the lining panels. This helped to speed up cleaning. Totalling 65, the Mk V Regents added distinction to an already distinctive fleet.

Tasteless designs

That trend toward lightweight buses had spawned some tasteless double-deck body designs. Most enthusiasts of the day, and some professional bus

people, too, winced at the sight of the five-bay Metropolitan-Cammell-Weymann Orion. It had a frameless front dome and a top-heavy appearance resulting from the relatively shallow upstairs windows. Some examples had no beading between panels. Where ultra-lightweight was specified (and it could be as low as 46cwt) the interior finish was severely spartan. During the 1936-50 period, Rochdale Corporation had bought more than 50 new bodies from the Weymann side of the MCW organisation. Unlike many others, however, the Lancashire town did not take any examples of the Orion body but continued to specify the Weymann medium-weight design of more traditional appearance and in this case, four-bay construction. Other features included equal-size windows, framed front dome and pleasantly-curving profiles at both rear and front. Thirty of H33/26R pattern were delivered in 1953/4 on Daimler CVG6 chassis, followed over the years to 1959 by a further 55 on AEC Regent V.

All 85 chassis sported tin fronts. The Daimler version, as seen also on Guy and Crossley chassis,

Left: *The 'deliciously extravagant' Massey features of the 1948-54 period show clearly in this view of Sunderland Corporation no.98 (GR 9930), a 1948 Daimler CVG6 on which the 'LNER streamlined Pacific profile' style of livery echoes the lines of the body. It can be clearly seen how this body evolved into the Birkenhead style.* W. J. Haynes

differed from the AEC example by being a little narrower and deeper, also having a less widely-arched top. A chromium-plated eyebrow-shaped motif at the top of the grille was meant to perpetuate the long-established fluting that characterised Daimler bus and car radiator shells. The shapeliness of the Weymann body seemed well-matched to the tin front which itself had been conceived during the period when British motor car styling was turning toward more integrated, flowing and indeed bulbous features.

Rochdale's Weymann-bodied Gardner-engined Daimlers were numbered 238-52 (JDK 738 etc) and 253-67 (KDK 653 etc) and were the first new buses in the fleet for two years. They were among the earliest Daimler CVG6s to have the left-hand preselector 'gate' change lever, superseding the right-hand quadrant arrangement. From 1950, Gardner had marketed the 'K' version of its LW range of engines. This offered increased power output without loss of fuel economy. On the 6LW the figure went up from 102 to 112bhp at the usual governed engine speed of 1,700rpm (figures that seem puny by current standards!). Rochdale, however, specified that the engines in its Daimlers should be adjusted to give the original output of 102bhp for improved fuel consumption.

Distinctive livery

The Rochdale livery of those times was among the most distinctive of any in the country. It comprised a medium-dark blue with a contrasting ivory, and black

horizontal beadings. The blue was applied in 1930s-style streamline fashion with downsweeping at the front of the upper saloon panelling on each side. The destination aperture layout at the front followed the pattern of Manchester Corporation (a joint operator with Rochdale on some services) and scored high for clarity. Advertisements were not carried. When in the 1960s Rochdale changed its livery to ivory with one blue band (at cantrail-level) the buses seemed bland by comparison.

Internally, the Weymann bodies had pressed aluminium window finishers similar to those seen inside most (but not all) Orions. They were painted blue and, with the blue leathercloth trim of the seats, reminded one of some 1930s trams. The handsome appearance of these Daimlers could have been improved perhaps only by the fitting of the traditional chromium-plated radiator shell but this was no longer available.

Arab IV

One chassis on which the Birmingham-style tin front was standard and the exposed radiator optional was the Guy Arab Mk IV. This model had been developed for Birmingham Corporation in 1949 but did not finally supersede the Mk III in production until four years later. Guy Arabs of the Mk II and III variety with Gardner 5LW or 6LW engines (which comprised the vast majority, compared with those powered by Meadows engines) had a bonnet and radiator that projected several inches forward of the dash panelling, creating a 'snout' effect. With the usual forward-

sweeping of the front edges of the wings, too, the overall appearance of the model was not attractive, no matter what the make of bodywork. The Mk IV with exposed radiator was a vast improvement in this respect. There was virtually no projection at the front. The rear of the radiator tended to line up with the dash and this resulted in a much neater and less clumsy-looking effect. Tastefully-shaped wings without a forward sweep at the front added to the appeal.

In peacetime, Guy tended to be a minority make among northwest England municipalities as a whole. However, one of the few that did take a relatively high proportion was Birkenhead. This operator bought 67 Guys, representing some 40% of the intake of new double-deckers between 1946 and 1956. Of those, 47 were bodied by the Wigan-based concern, Massey Bros. Among these, 17 were Mk IVs. Now, there was a stylish combination!

The Massey concern had been building bus bodies since 1920. During the mid-1930s it began to produce a distinctive double-deck design with good proportions and an easily recognisable upper deck front. This was characterised by widely-radiused outer upper corners and square lower ones to the upstairs front windows. Over the years to 1939 this kind of styling was developed until a design incorporating many 'streamline' features evolved. These details included 'D'-shaped foremost and rearmost lower saloon side windows, a pleasantly raked and curving frontal profile, and even wider radii to the upper outer corners of those windows at the front of the upper saloon. After the wartime utility interruption the theme was resumed from late 1945. It reached its culmination during the 1948-54 period when almost all Massey highbridge double-deck bodies appeared with deliciously extravagant curving features that clearly harked back to the era of the 'streaks' on the LNE and LMS railways. (Lowbridge versions, however, had an almost grotesque frontal rake.)

Timber-framed

Massey Bros' bodies had almost all been timber-framed, although a small minority had been built with

optional metal frames and indeed Birkenhead bought one of those in 1950. Regrettably, many operators had to rebuild their Massey wooden-framed bodies about halfway through their expected life span (although in fairness the same could be said about other makes of the same era using timber structure). From 1954, the standard Massey framing was metal and a high-quality product it was, too. At the same time, the windows at the front of the upper saloon lost their somewhat exaggerated upper outer corner radii and the 'D'-shaping of the windows at each end of the lower saloon ceased. A strong hint of streamlining still remained, however. It could be seen in the illusory slight widening of the upper saloon front corners toward the top together with their real graceful curve backward. Perhaps the only discordant note about the Massey design of body for forward-engined chassis was the somewhat high front bulkhead waistrail. On a low-bonneted chassis like the Arab III and IV the waistrail could have been lower by about 8in or so, greatly improving the view forward from downstairs seats.

Birkenhead's Massey-bodied Arab IVs were nos.355-61 (DCM 975-81) and nos.372-81 (EBG 59-64, 750-3), all H31/28R, new in 1955 and 1956 respectively and powered by the Gardner 6LW engine. The standard Birkenhead livery was a charming medium-light blue with a relieving cream band at upper saloon waistrail level and cream cantrail and lower saloon window surrounds. Indicator apertures were somewhat large, as in next-door Wallasey, and seemed to add distinction. Internally, the seats were trimmed with blue leathercloth-type material rather like Rochdale's. The exciting visual impression created by these buses was matched by the aural treats within. These came

mostly from the constant-mesh gearbox which entertained passengers with melodious euphony through the ratios. Most of Birkenhead's Guys operated from New Ferry depot and ran on some fairly hilly terrain where much intermediate gear work was necessary. It was in such situations that the orchestration of the 'box was heard to best effect. Neither were these buses just a pretty sight and sound. The combination of the tough, dependable Guy Arab and the durable, well-built Massey body resulted in an eminently serviceable and trouble-free vehicle.

Most ungainly

Leyland's tin front was probably the most ungainly of those to be seen. In overall appearance it reminded one of a somewhat all-embracing garment, perhaps like Queen Victoria's skirts, made worse by vertical slots of unequal length. The original had been developed for Midland Red and the slots were arranged in order to accommodate that operator's badge toward the top. Leyland didn't take the trouble to do a simple bit of redesigning for the many tin-fronted Titans ordered by other concerns. The alternative exposed radiator shell was preferable, although this lacked the elegance of the chromium-plated AEC and Daimler articles and the neatness of the Guy. Nevertheless, it was functional and of course a familiar sight throughout much of Britain. Among the best-looking postwar Leyland 'deckers, I suggest, were the 1953 PD2/14s of Leeds City Transport. There were only 10 of these, a small batch for such a large concern, numbered 301-10 (RNW 301 etc).

The 7ft 6in wide PD2/14 was in effect a provincial version of the London RTL. As with the AEC Regent

Left: *Throughout the whole peacetime period from the early 1930s the grace and charm of Roe double-deck bodywork as fitted to front-engined chassis was not confined to frontal and side features, as demonstrated here by the smooth back end of Selnec PTE no.5427 (227 YTB), a 1962 Leyland Titan PD2/40, still carrying the livery and fleetnumber of its former owner, Ashton-under-Lyne Corporation.*
John Fozard

III which was the edition of the RT for the provinces, the low bonnet and radiator of the London models was not incorporated. The steering column, moreover, was less upright than on the capital's versions and there were other non-London features under the surface. Leeds's order for PD2/14s represented the only examples of this Titan variant to be built. (There were no 8ft-wide specimens at all.) Transmission was through the AEC preselective gearbox with characteristic selector lever on the left of the steering column. The H33/25R bodywork with standard 'safety' staircase was built by Chas H. Roe of Leeds and to that concern's Pullman style introduced in 1948, although this variation was not specified by all customers initially.

From 1936, Roe had been building double-deck bodies with an elegantly-curving frontal outline. This was resumed after the war and, as happened with most other builders, details were gradually refined. The Pullman design incorporated deeper windows to both saloons. Of course, deeper upstairs windows meant shallower upper saloon panelling and this seemed to balance the general proportions even better than with the existing attractive design. Nothing was exaggerated or over-stated. The overall appearance was that of a bus that was both handsome and sturdy. Internally, some 'Pullman' bodies had wood trim around the windows. Others, including these on Leeds's PD2/14s, had metal finishers.

Leeds had placed in service nearly 200 AEC Regents of the Mk III variety with preselectors during 1947-52. It seemed almost natural for this Leyland order to be for the PD2/14, even though Leeds was also running 60 synchromesh PD2/1 Titans at that time.

Understandably, the PD2/14 sounded and behaved somewhat like a London RTL. Drivers found them heavy on the steering, by all accounts, but enthusiasts looked on them as 'a lovely bus'. The Leyland O.600 type 9.8litre engine was usually a little more subdued than its AEC 9.6 counterpart and, to audiences unaccustomed to RTL travel, it was probably curious to hear the whooping and gulping of the preselective 'box and fluid transmission in conjunction with the subdued roar of the O.600 (which in the PD2/14 could be heard just a little more than in the RTL). The smooth take-up from rest was also a change from the usual Leyland clutch-judder! These 10 unusual Leylands looked smart in the sober, not to say sombre, Leeds livery of two-tone green. When they were new, the lighter shade embraced the single area of the lower saloon window window-surrounds and the cantrail-level band. Subsequently, however, it was restricted to the cantrail contour only. This did nothing to brighten up appearances. A single large aperture housed two blinds, the upper one for the destination and the lower, large one for the route and service number. At the front of the canopy, alongside the top of the left-hand cab pillar, there was a small indicator which could be illuminated to show 'Limited' for operation on fast services. These features, along with the unpainted bonnet, were characteristically 'Leeds' and made the city's buses that little bit extra special.

There were, of course, other bonny buses of the same period. The few double-deck examples I have recalled are just a selection. I hope they illustrate a broad cross-section of what could be seen and heard in the transport arena of 45 years ago. **CB**

SIXTY YEARS ON

PHILIP MOUNTFORD looks back to North Staffordshire in the 1930s and early 1940s

IN THE summer of 1935 I left the little local school near my home to attend a Church School in the centre of Newcastle-under-Lyme on the outskirts of the Potteries. Newcastle was, and still is, an independent borough with a long history, which has never become part of its larger neighbour, Stoke-on-Trent, whose boundaries come within about half a mile of Newcastle town centre.

Then my life changed. My fascination for numbers and dates was transferred to the buses I saw and used on my twice-daily journeys to school – a mile each way morning and afternoon. Rather like the geometrical problems which we worked out in mathematics lessons at Newcastle High School in later years, it was a question of 'Given', 'To Prove' and 'Proven'. I was pleased to find, long afterwards, when reference books became available, that most of what I had worked out was accurate.

By September 1935 I had acquired a few basic facts. I knew the Potteries trams were withdrawn in 1928, so the largest batch of buses, QLs nos.102-51, dated from that time. I knew the local vehicle registrations were EH and VT for Stoke-on-Trent and RE and RF for Staffordshire county. To an observant eye it was soon clear VT followed EH and was itself followed by AEH, AVT, BEH and BVT. CEH was then the current Stoke-on-Trent mark. I also knew that besides PMT, still referred to by older people as PET (Potteries Electric Traction became known as Potteries Motor Traction in 1933), there were many small local bus owners. A cousin drove for Rowley's.

The only tools of the trade were the 64-page penny PMT timetable, which was published several times a year, and the free *Touring Handbook*, both obtainable from the bus office in Percy Street, Hanley, right beside the Newcastle bus terminus. The timetables, now collectors' items, contained a rudimentary map of the area, also showing the names and territories of adjacent company operators – Crosville, North Western, Trent and Midland Red. The cover design featured a 1935 Leyland coach. The *Handbook*, issued in 1936, contained a potted history of the company and an excellent photograph of no.96, a Burlingham-bodied saloon, which saw regular service on my local route. To my regret I never kept these booklets but have since obtained copies from a London dealer.

Memory

In those early days I never kept written records. I never considered it necessary. Even today, 60 years later, my memory for names, addresses, dates and numbers is as good as ever. Nevertheless I now regret not having done so, especially with regard to buses I saw only briefly on holidays in North Wales and the Fylde of Lancashire. My travels before and during the war years were of necessity limited to a comparatively small area of England and Wales.

My earliest recollections, apart from the 'toastracks' of Colwyn Bay and the trams of Lytham St Annes and Blackpool, were the high-stepped red SOS FS or Q types of Potteries buses, on which I travelled once a week on the long circular service (later service 29), familiarly known as the 'Riley Arms'. This destination was in those days an out-of-the-way hostelry in High Lane, Tunstall, but served as an identification for this complex hour-long route through residential districts of Stoke and Newcastle which were not well served by other buses. This took me from my school at May Bank to Hartshill where

POTTERIES
MOTOR TRACTION CO. LTD.

The
OFFICIAL HANDBOOK
WITH MAP

my grandparents lived. I particularly remember the awkward 'half step' on these vehicles of 1926-7 vintage. Later this route was served by 1930 CODs, identifiable by having cream tops as opposed to the usual silver shade. In September 1935, when I changed schools, I started to use buses daily. St Giles' and St George's School was happily still standing on the occasion of my

Top: *Potteries no.19 (EH 3423), a Daimler Y of 1922 with Brush body. This bus was withdrawn in 1930.*
All photos from P. H. Mountford collection

Above: *Probably the earliest type of bus the author travelled on – Potteries no.44 (EH 4941), a 1924 Brush-bodied Tilling-Stevens (though the radiator suggests an SOS). It survived until 1934.*

last visit to my home town. Though it was only a penny bus ride from Basford where I lived, it was usual to walk to school downhill, and ride on the bus uphill home. I soon found myself taking an interest in the fleet and registration numbers and rapidly began piecing together the jigsaw. As time went on, I travelled to school earlier and spent more and more time in Nelson Place, Newcastle, where six busy roads met, watching the movements of buses during the morning rush-hour. This was a time of rapid change in the industry and I was able to survey a vast and varied

Top: A typical North Staffs independent. A Baxter of Hanley Leyland-bodied Tiger of 1931, possibly VT 5743.

Above: Peake's (North Stafford Motors) only double-decker, VT 8363, an all-Leyland Titan TD2 of 1932. This became Associated no.5 in 1939 and PMT no.505 in 1944. It survived until 1946, spending most of its life on the Stoke-Newcastle route.

array of buses dating from 1926 vehicles soon destined for scrap, to 1936's streamlined saloons in PMT's highly individual style, and the numerous independent

operators' luxury coaches of which Willowbrook designs predominated.

The Basford route, 1A (service numbers were never displayed before 1936) from Hanley to Newcastle, had a 12min headway during most of the day, and a six-minute peak service. A. R. Smedler of Hartshill, whose solitary bus was housed at a garage in Albert Street, Newcastle, operated VT 8219, a dark green Dennis Lancet, on a regular schedule in the morning and evening and all day Saturday. The same two conductors with badge numbers DD1004 and DD5151 worked on his bus from 1935 (perhaps much earlier) until take-over in 1939, and long afterwards in ABC or PMT service. Smedler operated the 4.36pm trip from Newcastle to Basford and as I could not use my 'contract' on his vehicle, I was allowed to use PMT's 71 Burslem service to May Bank instead. This involved a much longer walk, so after a few weeks I regularly used this much-loved green bus, paying the penny fare. I have never seen a photograph of this vehicle. It had a Duple body with a predominantly white interior and lasted until July 1937 when it was replaced by EVT 701, another Dennis with Willowbrook coachwork, which became Associated no.19 and PMT no.519. I never saw VT 8219 again.

The other buses on the Basford service were all PMT except for an elderly Associated Leyland which worked the route on Sundays. In 1935 there was one SOS QL, one COD and a Leyland Tiger of the nos.56-85 batch which I soon realised were then the newest Potteries vehicles. It was PMT policy to spread its newer vehicles round the system so each route tended to have buses of different types and ages. A QL of 1928 operated the 12.36pm trip on which I travelled home for lunch, and a modern Leyland the 12.48pm which I occasionally used.

Main classes

I soon worked out the main classes of Potteries buses. It was obvious that the oldest and largest main group,

PMT no.153 (VT 2505), an SOS 'Madam' of 1929 with Brush body. This was sold to Bunce of Worthen, Shropshire, outliving most of the rest of the batch of 25.

the SOS QLs nos.l02-51 (VT 801-50) were bought in 1928 to replace the trams; the halfcab Leylands nos.56-85 (BEH 956-85) were the newest, of 1935 vintage. Those in between I accurately assigned to the correct year but there was no means of knowing that the 1931 SOS IM4s actually first operated with PMT's subsidiaries like Morton or Proctor, of whom I had no knowledge. There were still a few vehicles of 1927 vintage – I remember seeing HA-registered no.90 in Bagnall Street, Newcastle, a bus which came from Midland Red, but the main batches were the SOS QLs of 1928; the Ms of 1929; nos.152-76 (VT 2501-25 – not all in that order); the CODs of 1930, with more comfortable interiors and net luggage-racks; nos.201-21 (VT 4501-21); then the IM4s of 1931, nos.13-22 (VT 6151-60), and identical vehicles of 1932 (VT 7901-6). The latter had mixed fleetnumbers.

Later in 1932 came four double-deckers, the first since the very early days of the company. Nos.27-30 (VT 8601-4) were also SOS vehicles, which to me were the norm. I learned that they were built by Midland Red at Birmingham, from whom many elderly vehicles were hired by PMT for factory services during the war years. A small 1933 intake of five Leyland double-deckers followed, nos.23-6 and 31 (VT 9701-5) but except for one more Leyland, the 1934 batch were again SOS, all but one of these double-deckers: nos.231-247 (AVT 551-567). No.231 was the solitary Leyland, no.247 (later no.227) an SOS coach. By then there were still only 25 double-decker vehicles operating for PMT – all of the lowbridge type, a necessity in a hilly area with a complexity of railway lines. The SOS deckers seemed of unrobust appearance and their life on heavily-loaded trunk

routes caused their premature demise. Some did not last through the war years.

The 1932 saloons were numbered 32, 33, 35, 38, 179 and 181. This typified PMT's gap-filling policy. Buses numbered up to 10 or between 177 and 200 were usually of secondhand origin, some numbers being used several times in a few years. Many were of Tilling-Stevens manufacture, a type much favoured by the smaller independents for financial reasons. In the late 1930s they were used mainly only at peak times and on works services but there were plenty in evidence in Nelson Place. No two were quite the same and a few operated with 'A' suffixes after their fleetnumbers had been given to new 1936 Leylands. It was quite obvious that their bodies were very basic in design and comfort.

Licence plates

My perceptive eye had also noticed the local authority

Top: *Probably one of PMT's 1933 Leylands, nos.23-6 (VT 9701-4) – though no.231 (AVT 551) of 1934 was identical.*

Above: *One of several Willowbrook-bodied Leylands of 1937-9 vintage in the Associated fleet. All saw service with PMT, some receiving coach livery.*

licence plates, black figures on small white ovals on the backs of the vehicles, the weights of the buses, which varied from 4ton 14cwt for the IM4s to over six tons for the newer saloons, and the bodybuilders' plates, of which Weymann, Brush and Willowbrook were the most familiar.

In the new year of 1936 PMT put 36 fine new vehicles into service, registered CVT 1-36. The first few were Leyland double-deckers nos.252-61, long-lived, later rebodied and renumbered. No.55 was a

Above: **Two PMT double-deckers with similar Brush bodies demonstrate the antiquated look of the 1932 SOS REDD (no.29, VT 8603 on the left) compared to the 1933 Leyland Titan TD3 (no.26, VT 9704). Both buses saw heavy service in the war years, surviving until 1948 and 1949 respectively.**

luxury coach which I rarely saw; the rest were single-deck saloons, one AEC (no.100), one Daimler (no.101, always my favourite) and 23 Leylands nos.86-95 with Weymann coachwork, nos.96-9 Burlingham and nos.186-95 Brush. All of these were elaborately finished and upholstered in a highly individual style and all had outside luggage racks. The basic design was the same but the details and the shape of the cream streamline stripes varied according to the bodybuilder. The Weymann-built vehicles originally had non-standard fleet numbers of a plainer more modern style. Otherwise fleet numbers conformed to tramway type numerals until a simplified style was adopted during the war. Three more Daimlers (nos.102-4) followed in mid-1936.

From 1937 until 1940 similar batches of new buses appeared, both single- and double-deckers, Daimler vehicles playing an increasingly important part. From 1939 the luggage racks were absent. The 1940 Willowbrook batch, 176-80 (HVT 296-300), were in my opinion the best-looking vehicles ever operated by PMT, with maroon added to the normal red and cream livery. This was short-lived. No.178 received an all-over khaki camouflage. Most other buses were given grey tops. Most of PMT's saloons of the late 1930s were what would these days be called dual-purpose. Large numbers of them would be needed for use during the August 'Wakes Week' mass-migration. Dozens of buses would make two return trips to Blackpool on the busiest August Saturdays when normal town services would be cut to the absolute minimum.

To me it was normal practice for batches of new vehicles to go into service at the very beginning of the year. Certainly in 1937 and 1938 new buses were running on 1 January, not then a public holiday. In 1939 the single-deckers came a bit later.

Numbering system

In prewar days PMT's numbering system was straightforward. It was consecutive with both complete batches and individual numbers being re-used. By 1936 it had reached no.261, nos.262-6 coming officially at the end of 1936, though I did not see them until the New Year. Nos.267-93 arrived in 1937. For the next three years old numbers were re-used, then in 1942 a batch of long 8ft wide Daimlers, diverted from Rhodesia, took the score to no.300. Further wartime deliveries of 'utility' deckers reached no.342, though from 1944 ex-Associated vehicles appeared in PMT wartime colours (red and grey) with 500 added to their ABC fleet numbers.

The lowest fleetnumber regularly seen was no.13, an IM4 (VT 6151), the numbers below that were rarities – subjects of fleeting glimpses. Some were coaches like the normal-control nos.7 and 8 acquired from Lewis of

Cheswardine, Shropshire, in 1936. Others were ordinary saloons. The only No.1 I ever saw was a 1930 Leyland Lion which originated with Knight's of Hanley and later passed to Brown's. No.3 was an ancient Leyland PLSC from Biddulph & District, retained for school and works services; nos.9 and 10 were renumbered TSMs. Nos.11 and 12 were a rare pair of Burlingham coachwork SOS saloons of 1930 which were rebodied – not then normal PMT practice – having been charabancs originally.

Numbers had only reached 151 by 1928, 176 by 1929, 226 in 1930 and 247 by 1934. Several independents were taken over in 1929 which explains why so many 'odd' vehicles had numbers between 177 and 200.

The large batch of 1935 Leyland saloons (there were also five luxury coaches, later painted red, white and blue and known as 'Coronation Coaches,' numbered 222, 223, 228, 229 and 230), replaced a similarly large batch of 1925 SOS S buses, taking their numbers 56-85. Further batches of SOS vehicles were then replaced each year until the war. The QLs went by the end of 1937, the Ms at the end of 1938 and most of the CODs by 1940. Some of the latter were converted to ambulances and a few survived the war. The numerical progression seemed logical and orderly but for reasons unknown nos.121-3 remained unused after the demise of the QLs. Nos.121 and 122 were later used in wartime for 'unfrozen' Leylands, but no.123 was never reallocated until the major renumbering of 1953.

In 1935 I soon became aware that a batch of QLs,

Above: This Albion CX13 of 1939 with Lawton body, HRE 139, spent most of its life on Rowley's Stoke-Newcastle route and its later extensions. It became PMT no.S491 in 1954, surviving only one year in this guise.

nos.39-54, were odd in that they carried CC (Caernarvonshire) registrations. I did not know until much later that these came from Llandudno Blue (Royal Blue) via Crosville.

Take-over

PMT, over the years, had acquired many small bus operators, but from 1936 until almost the end of World War 2, only one further take-over occurred, that of Lymer of Blythe Bridge in 1939. At the extreme south-eastern end of the Potteries, this was unknown territory to me at the time, but I saw some of Lymer's handsome vehicles elsewhere in PMT's short-lived dark blue coach livery.

Then in 1944 came the important merger with Associated Bus Companies of Hanley and the lesser acquisition of the picturesque Newcastle-Eccleshall route of Bradley, though not his worn-out vehicles.

Associated (ABC) was by far the largest of the numerous North Staffordshire independents, of which at one time there were over 70. One of several such associations or partnerships originally, it expanded considerably in 1939 taking over besides Smedler's single vehicle, the green Dennis of Garbett & Bonnett,

Above: *PMT no.101 (CVT 36), the solitary Daimler (COG5) in a batch of 36 new vehicles which entered service early in 1936. Three similar Daimlers, nos.102-4, arrived later in that year.*

which ran between Newcastle and Silverdale, and a colourful array of 'Main Route' operators. The main Longton to Tunstall route linked the six Potteries towns (Arnold Bennett forgot Fenton, the smallest of the six and has never really been forgiven for his lapse) by a two-minute service requiring about 75 vehicles at peak times. Barker operated a dark blue Leyland, CEH 182, Kent had a bright red Leyland, FVT 897 with a Willowbrook body, seemingly a favourite combination, C. & S. Eaton had two green and beige Dennises, McMinn (strictly two separate businesses for legal reasons) several red or maroon Leylands, Cartwright a single Duple-bodied Leyland, DEH 711, which I only remember seeing once, Hill two pale blue and cream Leylands and Peake (North Stafford Motors) a larger fleet of about 20 Leylands in a grey and dark blue livery. 'North Stafford' operated a much more extensive network than the other operators taken over by Associated, running as far as Alsager and Crewe, over the Cheshire boundary.

The first I knew of the 1939 take-overs was the appearance of small black fleet numbers on the fronts of the buses involved. Smedler's Dennis became no.19 in the ABC fleet. Most of these survived long after PMT took over, two 1938 models remaining in service until 1957.

Apart from Smedler's buses, the 'independent' I knew best was Peake's VT 8363, a 1932 Leyland, at one time the only double-decker in the area not then owned by PMT, which always operated on the Newcastle-Stoke route. Originally in a grey and green livery, it became standard grey and blue before becoming ABC no.5, running in its cream and red livery for most of the war years. Thereafter it was PMT

no.505 so I knew this vehicle in four different guises.

Liveries

ABC itself changed its liveries frequently. In 1935 the older vehicles were light brown, the newer green and cream. Later an elaborate colour-scheme of yellow, maroon, cream and red was adopted. This was simplified about 1939 and eventually Associated buses appeared in PMT's standard wartime colours of red and grey.

There were numerous other independent operators, from the Big Five: Mainwaring, Brown, Tilstone, Stoke Motors and Milton Bus Company, all of which became part of PMT in 1951-2, to small proprietors like Rowley and Davies which lasted a few more years. One, Procter, still survives, operating from Hanley to Leek via Cellarhead on route 16. This, I believe, is the only unchanged 1930s route to retain its original number. But that is another story.

By 1945, at the end of the war, I was able to widen my travels, seeing ancient SOS vehicles of Midland Red – far older than anything PMT still ran – when on a cycling holiday in Worcestershire, equally ancient Eastern Counties Tillings in Cambridge and a wide and colourful variety of old buses, including Young's Albions in their attractive orange and maroon livery, when I visited my aunt in the west of Scotland. The buses of the Potteries, though, remained my first love. **CB**

CHECKPOINT

No.1: Ribble's PD3s

Born: Preston, Lancashire September 1957.

Parents: Ribble Motor Services and the Ministry of Transport. The MoT had authorised operation of two-axle 30ft double-deckers from July 1957 and Ribble was one of the first BET group companies to take advantage of this new concession, starting with chassis number 570556, the sixth Leyland Titan PD3 to be built.

Was this its only claim to fame?: By no means. When it upgraded itself from shorter PD2s to PD3s, Ribble also switched to a forward-entrance layout with a power-operated sliding door. Sliding doors enjoyed some favour elsewhere, but in nothing like the quantities that Ribble took, and Ribble also was the first UK operator to turn its back on rear-entrance buses. For ever.

Their only distinguishing feature?: No. Another was that all 236 PD3s bought new by Ribble had full fronts, a feature that anticipated the imminent move by Ribble and others to rear-engined buses, so they were meant to look more modern than the buses the company had bought until then.

Unique to Ribble?: No. Southdown followed suit with its even more numerous Queen Marys; and others, Blackpool to name but one, also preferred full fronts. Nor, incidentally, were they Ribble's first fully-fronted double-deckers; the White Lady semi-coach PD1s and PD2s had introduced them in 1949/50, but the PD3s were the first mainstream machines to have them.

All done by one bodybuilder?: All done by two. The first 105, on manual gearbox PD3/4 chassis, were bodied by Burlingham in 1957/58; the other 131 had Metro-Cammell Weymann bodies on semi-automatic PD3/5 chassis and arrived in 1961-3. In between, and in parallel with some of the later deliveries, Ribble bought big batches of early rear-engined Atlanteans.

What was behind their unusual specification?: A desire to make the most of the new length limit. Like other urban and inter-urban operators, Ribble was being hit by rising operating costs and shortages of staff, so 72-seat PD3s had space for 11 more passengers than their immediate predecessors. On the other hand, they were a shade more expensive to operate, so it was essential that all 11 extra passengers' fares were collected along with those that sometimes went uncollected on a PD2. The forward entrance meant the driver could supervise boarding and alighting and leave the conductor free to sell tickets. The full front made it possible to omit glazing from the bulkhead behind the driver, and cut out reflections.

Did this work?: Given that 236 were bought over six years

and they lived full lives, we can assume that the answer probably was yes. But they had their critics, not the least of whom was T. A. Dalton, the *Buses Illustrated* columnist, who penned a less than complimentary assessment of them in the January 1958 issue, soon after the first examples went into service in Carlisle. He worried about drivers getting stiff necks from turning to supervise the entrances, disliked their spiral staircases, argued that conductors would have to collect 80 fares in four minutes if the buses were to work properly, and said the lack of bulkhead glazing would cause the windscreen to steam up. He reckoned they were better suited to inter-urban duties, and Ribble certainly did run them on just that sort of route.

Any other claims to fame?: The last 36, the TCKs of 1963, made history by being the first double-deckers built to the recently authorised 8ft 2.5in (2.5m) width limit. Indeed, they remained the only full-width double-deckers for quite a few years. Ribble certainly was determined to be prepared for the future.

Like the Scouts?: Perhaps, but not like Scout Motor Services of Preston. It sold out to Ribble in 1962 and with it came five more Burlingham-bodied PD3 halfcabs otherwise very similar to the 105 original full-fronts. The oldest pair had an unusual past as they started life on the Leyland factory floor as PD2s and were lengthened into PD3s before being bodied.

Life after Ribble?: The Burlinghams began to be withdrawn around 1973/74 and several were acquired by independents. Cunningham of Paisley, with six, was one to use them for further stage carriage work. But the most unlikely new home for 20 similar KCKs and LCKs surfaced in 1975/76 when London Country took them for manual gearbox driver training in place of preselective RTs, repainted them yellow and gave them fleetnumbers LR1-20.

The end?: The last nine – from all three MCW-bodied batches – survived with Ribble until late-September 1981; by then, new-fangled creations like Olympians and National 2s were arriving. **ALM**

The first of Ribble's 105 1957/8 Leyland Titan PD3/4s with Burlingham 72-seat bodies.

MEMORIES OF ATHOL STREET

TED SHEPHERD remembers life as a conductor in one of London's smaller depots

SOME long-closed London Transport bus garages have faded into history, and perhaps relatively few readers today will recall Putney Bridge, Old Kent Road or West Green from the good old days of late 1940s and early 1950s London. However, one such garage, long demolished, still lives on by reputation, if not in bricks and mortar. It was a small garage by London's standards, its buses didn't penetrate the famous parts of the city, and they spent a sizeable proportion of their day below ground on routes through the Blackwall and Rotherhithe Tunnels. That garage was Athol Street.

Athol Street was located in a cul-de-sac close to the main A13 East India Dock Road, Poplar, and had originally been purchased in 1879 as a horse-bus yard. It was adjacent to the shed and stables of the North Metropolitan Tramways Company. It was over 40 years since the last horse had gone that I was allocated to the garage in 1950 as a trainee conductor. I regarded myself lucky that it was Athol Street, it being the easiest to get to from home, and the routes operated seemed to offer an interest that others lacked. Incidentally, Athol Street was paralleled by Blair Street, but Blair Atholl must have had first claim upon the spelling!

My instructor, Wally, was a one-time union representative and knew the job inside out. Wally did not follow me around but let me get on with the job of collecting fares, and was always there if any problem arose. Athol Street's chief depot inspector was a kindly man who put me at ease straight away, but he was in poor health and soon retired. The other depot inspectors were mostly helpful and easy to get on with.

The conditions in which the inspectors worked were decidedly cramped, being in a timber structure located in a corner of the garage, and bedecked in olive green paint. The canteen was very basic with its wooden chairs and tables, the latter having heavy white enamel tops. The rough stone floor, which was bare, was a feature and it reminds me of a driver named Frank who worked on the 108s. Frank was a practical joker and would, on occasion, when most were busy tackling a meal or deep in conversation, spin a china dinner plate on the floor. As the plate stopped spinning there would be a deafening racket while it rolled around before settling on the floor. Frank would also often be heard to blow a shrill blast on a whistle when on his way through the nearby tunnels.

Above: **Ted Shepherd at the wheel of a RTL1050 a bus that was garaged at Athol Street from 1950 until 1955, at the 1993 Holloway garage London Transport diamond jubilee open day.**
David Thrower

Friendly garage

An advantage that Athol Street (code letter C) possessed was its homeliness, being one of the smallest in the Central (red bus) Area. It was easy to get to know one's workmates, especially as being a new man you were on the 'spare' list and worked with an assortment of drivers. Often you would start a week on the early shift but before the weekend you could be on lates again, there being then no ruling on shifts as was introduced in later years. Another aspect of being new was that you could be loaned to any one of about a dozen garages to work an assortment of routes. Although I knew my way around most of London it could be very confusing in the busy spells, especially at night and in poorly-lit areas. The large Dagenham and Becontree estates were particularly difficult, with so many roads almost indistinguishable from one another.

There was no provision for conductors to 'learn the road' as there was for drivers, and it was to be some years before conductors were to be given time with pay to familiarise themselves with a particular route. A couple of late shifts on Saturdays on loan to the 6 and 106 out of Hackney (Well Street) garage almost had me handing in my notice. The 22 out of the same

garage could be a teaser, too, especially on a wet day with many passengers riding even the shortest distance; conductors on each deck would have had plenty to occupy them. Although these routes were mostly worked with prewar STLs, the RTs, RTLs and RTWs were appearing in increasing numbers and I had the pleasure of working on the 10 from Victoria (GM) garage to Woodford Bridge on four consecutive days with newly-delivered RTs.

But back to Athol Street. The 56 route served the Isle of Dogs and was the only service on the island by this time. Previously, for many years, there had been two separate routes, both terminating at Cubitt Town from opposite directions. Originally the 57, which must have been one of the shortest in London, came from Blackwall Tunnel, while the 56 came in from Mile End station, but by the 1950s the 56 served the island throughout, but no longer went beyond Limehouse.

The 56, with terminals barely a mile apart along the A13, was a busy route for much of the time, the Isle of Dogs being a heavily industrialised area in addition to having two major dock complexes at Millwall and West

Left: **STL804 (BXD 463) stands outside Athol Street garage on 16 August 1951.**
Alan B. Cross

Below: **STL1881 on route 56 and a Tunnel STL on route 108 outside Woolmore Street School, which still stands today, on 1 April 1950. Woolmore Street was at that time the stand for route 56.**
Alan B. Cross

India/South West India. In the morning peak, buses would fill up at either terminus with people travelling on to the island to work and even more leaving for jobs elsewhere in London. A high frequency of service was needed and buses would be leaving at four-minute intervals at the height of the rush hour.

Top: *Tunnel STL1861 at the north end of the Blackwall Tunnel on 22 August 1952.*
Alan B. Cross

Above: *STL1607 on 1 April 1950 in a wonderful period East End setting, with what could be Steptoe and Son in the background.*
Alan B. Cross

One disturbing feature of the 56 was the excessive speeds at which buses were often driven. It was a delight for some crews to catch the bus in front, or at least get within sight of it. This would mean fewer people to pick up, and early running, with the reward of a longer layover at the terminus. More than once a warning was received from the local police about excessive speed and a notice would be posted up in the garage. As most of the roads on the island were granite setts they could also be extremely slippery when wet.

With at least three swing bridges operational in the early 1950s there were major hold-ups on the 56 when shipping was on the move, some of the longest delays being caused when a string of barges was being taken into or out of the docks. Some of the larger ocean-going vessels also meant a hold-up of 20min or more. With such delays it could mean that most of the buses were out of schedule by varying amounts and this called for quick thinking on the part of inspectors on the road to restore normality. Sometimes a bus would be turned back at each side of the bridge to maintain the service. Co-operation from the crews at these times was seldom lacking.

B type to RTL

However, the most distinctive routes that Athol Street worked, from their inception until the closure of the garage, were the three that ran beneath the Thames, via the Rotherhithe Tunnel (route 82) and the Blackwall Tunnel (routes 108 and 108A). The Blackwall Tunnel had opened as long ago as 1897, before the coming of the motor age, and the Rotherhithe Tunnel 11 years later. Until the 1960s, these two structures were the only road crossings east of Tower Bridge (itself vulnerable to delays from river traffic), and by the 1950s were a source of legendary congestion and not infrequent accidents.

Services through the Blackwall Tunnel had initially been provided by the redoubtable B type, in its single-deck form, later progressing to fearsome-looking NS types with unusual twin sunken gangways and 'knifeboard' longitudinal upper-deck seating, the downstairs having perimeter seating (it is a great pity that an example of these has not survived into preservation). These were replaced in 1937 with the well-known AEC STL13 class, the so-called 'Tunnel STLs', some 40 of which were based at Athol Street for almost all of their lives, but which by the late 1940s were approaching life expiry, hastened by the enforced neglect of wartime.

The Tunnel STLs were amongst the most attractive of all the sub-variants of the STL class, and their disappearance was mourned by the enthusiast world,

Below: *The author clearly remembers working RTL1042, seen here on 30 January 1954, on a Whipsnade excursion with a driver who apparently had difficulty changing down gear on hills for some unknown reason.*
Alan B. Cross

Above: *Tunnel STL1858 crosses the East India Dock Road and heads for the Blackwall Tunnel approach on 22 August 1952, with the Poplar Hospital in the background. The sign above the traffic light must have caused some head-scratching among drivers.*
Alan B. Cross

such as it was at the time. It is especially regrettable that one vehicle, STL 1871, survived with the independent Mulleys of Ixworth, Suffolk, sufficiently long afterwards to be bought for private preservation and restored, only to be sold for scrap after a couple of rally seasons.

In October 1950, the first batch of new Leyland RTLs arrived from temporary store at Edgware, for initial use on route 56, but with some further use on route 82 on Sundays. A further 10 buses arrived in March 1953 for the 108/108A, and RTLs gradually ousted the STLs in what was one of the most protracted changeovers of the STL/RT family metamorphosis. The 1950 batch were of interest in that they were the very last to carry the restricted wartime-type destination displays when delivered, this being another of Athol Street's idiosyncrasies.

In 1950 there were still a number of men who had been at Athol Street right back to the days of the NS, both standard and tunnel versions. A few had worked on single-deck S types which had preceded the NS and one driver I got to know just before he retired in his seventies had even been in at the start of the 56 with the B types in 1913. It is remarkable to think of starting your career with B-types and ending it with the luxury of an RTL!

As is widely known in enthusiast circles, one thing common to the STL and RTL buses operating on the tunnel services was that they were equipped with special tyres on the nearside, with reinforced walls in

order to stand up to the frequent rubbing against the kerbs within the tunnels. This was unavoidable when passing other large vehicles, the carriageways being only 16ft in width although the overall bore in Rotherhithe was slightly larger than that of the Blackwall, making room for wider footpaths. Some drivers preferred not to work on the tunnel routes, but chose to stay on the 56 working to the Isle of Dogs. It was also the probable reason why for many years no other garage was prepared to accept an allocation to operate on these subterranean routes. It is also not surprising to note that driver trainees were prohibited from the tunnels.

In the early postwar years, a special 'lowbridge RT' design had been contemplated but someone in the London Transport hierarchy had the courage to try out a pair of standard RTLs in October 1950 in the Blackwall Tunnel, confirming that a special 'Tunnel RT' would not be necessary. A test in the small hours with brand-new RTL896 and RTL899 confirmed a minimum clearance of 6in between their roof panels and the arched walls when passing each other at bends. Henceforth, standard STLs (until their

withdrawal), RTLs and eventually in the late 1960s, RTs were to operate routes through both tunnels, though RTWs of course remained excluded. Clearance for the revised arrangements was to be enhanced by the tyres, which are reputed to have lowered overall heights by a further inch.

New RTLs had arrived at Athol Street about a month before my arrival and were working the 56 in place of STLs. Some of these RTLs were to be seen at weekends on the 82, the other route working under the Thames via Rotherhithe Tunnel and still worked mainly with standard STLs on other days. The brand-new RTLs came to Athol Street in three initial batches, with 11 buses scattered between RTL889-1046 in September 1950, a further 11 between RTL 894-1050 the following month, then nine more (RTL1460-8 inclusive) in March 1953. A further quartet of 'new' buses numbered between RTL1598-1617 were unused buses that had been mothballed for four years, and which arrived in 1958 as part of cyclic overhauling, displacing existing identical vehicles. Many other secondhand buses, of course, were drafted in from other garages as part of this process, but Leylands maintained a monopoly from the end of the STL era until complete closure.

Routes beneath the river

The 82 route from Stepney East station to Rotherhithe via the Rotherhithe Tunnel served the Surrey Commercial Docks, a rather run-down area even more

isolated than the Isle of Dogs. This route too had three active swing bridges to contend with in those days, one being little more than 100yds from Surrey Docks station, renamed in recent years Surrey Quays. Timber was one of the main cargoes that used to arrive in this part of the docks, often on large vessels from such countries as Norway, Sweden, Finland and Russia, and lighters were used to distribute some of the cargoes to various yards. Some of the local residents in the Rotherhithe Street area became well-known to the bus crews, a number of whom had worked on the route for many years, and favours were often the order of the day, whether it was allowing the occasional free ride or stopping between recognised stops to pick up or set down a 'regular.' One driver told me that he once helped a family to move house by taking some furniture on board. This would have been during the very slack evening period when things were usually very quiet, especially at the weekends.

The 82 suited me up to a point as it was close to home, which I could reach even on a 40min meal break, but after a few months and up to 14 journeys a

day through the Rotherhithe Tunnel I decided on a change of tunnel(!) and put in for the 108s.

Officials responsible for the running of the 108/108A Blackwall Tunnel routes had their problems, often protracted, whenever a serious collision occurred that closed the tunnel for some considerable time. If caught in the resulting jam it could mean spending anything from 20min to an hour or two under the river while things were sorted out. The old-established London bus and coach operator Timpsons had a smart petrol-engined AEC Regal breakdown tender which was involved in a collision in mid-tunnel and was badly damaged. I never saw it again. Another major hold-up was caused when a loaded rigid eight-wheeler caught fire and was all but burned out 100yd or so from the north exit. On another occasion the stop-cock on a glucose tanker, which had not been secured, came undone and sprayed a stream of glutinous matter all through the tunnel. Firemen couldn't make much impression on it until the next day when it had hardened and could be chipped away.

Exhaust fumes were a real problem during busy times but when there was a stoppage most engines would be shut off and the atmosphere soon cleared. Things must have been much worse in the days before the installation of fans in the ventilation shafts on either side of the river section, and when steam wagons were allowed through. It was reputed that at one time staff on the 82, 108 and 108A were paid 4d a day 'milk money', in recognition of the health-damaging effects of repeatedly passing through the fumes below the river, although subsequent ventilation measures improved matters to some extent. The shortness of the 82 route meant that crews working it spent an appreciable part of their day below river.

Fog

I am also reminded of a time in late 1952 when a dense fog blacked out London and the southeast to such an extent that no buses, if memory serves me right, left the garage for a week. I don't know how other garages fared then but numbers of vehicles, including buses, were abandoned at the roadside, having run out of fuel or suffered flattened batteries after hours of idling in traffic. A driver who was on the 108 at the time, who retired in 1970, recently told me that on one journey he became stranded out on Blackheath, where he eventually had to spend the night. It's difficult to imagine being unable to see the ground at one's feet, let alone the kerb, with even walking a slow and hazardous process, especially at night.

The presence of a tram track would sometimes be of assistance in fog if it could be seen, and many a driver in previous years had followed a tram whilst it served

Above: **STL1841 on route 108A stands alongside Guy Arab utility/Northern Counties G294 on route 175 at the congested northern end of the Blackwall Tunnel on 22 August 1952.**
Alan B. Cross

the purpose, sometimes ending up at the depot! However, 1952 was the first winter without trams anywhere in London. On the 108 there had been trams immediately on reaching the south end of the tunnel where the 58 terminated after its lengthy run from Victoria. A short trip along the Woolwich Road was shared with the 36 and 38 on their way between Embankment and Abbey Wood, once a favourite Bank Holiday venue. Westcombe Hill then took the 108 away from the trams for the journey across Blackheath and through Lee Terrace to Lewisham, where trams were once in abundance. Here one met up with the 58 again which had come by way of Greenwich Church, a shorter route than that taken by the 108 bus.

From February 1951, the 108A was extended to Eltham, Southend Crescent, and was by that time operating throughout the day and evening with some peak-hour journeys to Well Hall Roundabout, but there were still some duties which did not involve a journey to Eltham. Likewise, there were certain duties when one would not see a journey through to Crystal Palace. When a journey to the latter was followed by one to Eltham or vice versa it meant that the whole blind display had to be changed.

A small but interesting point worth mentioning about the 82 and 108/108A routes is the use of wheel scotches. These were carried one to each bus, no doubt a ruling since the start of operations and well into the 1950s. Some readers may know of their use on various other routes which traversed hilly terrain. I well

remember them being used on the NSs in the 1930s where the 82 terminus at Stepney was on an incline just north of Rotherhithe Tunnel entrance. This arrangement continued until docks traffic created congestion problems and the stand was transferred to a point beneath Stepney East station, later renamed Limehouse prior to the opening of the Docklands Light Railway.

A brief interlude of interest was when RFs were used on a short section of the 108 over a brief period in about 1953 when the bridge over the District Railway line at Bromley-by-Bow was being reconstructed. Two or three RFs allocated from Dalston garage worked a shuttle between Devas Street on the south side of St Andrews Hospital and the 'Seven Stars', the ultimate northern terminus of the route, a few hundred yards further on, via a diversion under a very low bridge in Devons Road.

Though general maintenance in the tunnels was normally carried out at night, there were times when major repairs made it necessary for longer periods of closure, mainly at weekends. This usually meant a supplementary schedule and, in the case of the

Above: *Smart RTL364 picks up passengers at the Seven Stars public house at the Bromley-by-Bow terminus on 30 January 1954. The pub, but little else, remains unchanged today.*
Alan B. Cross

Blackwall Tunnel, buses going into service south of the river would go via Rotherhithe and make the long detour through Deptford and Greenwich. Relief crews due to take up service on the south side (Tunnel Avenue, 'Star in the East') would normally take the opportunity of travelling on these, the alternative being to walk through the tunnel. This took about 15min and was not unpleasant unless the work being carried out involved the use of pneumatic drills, when the effect in an enclosed space may well be imagined.

Other services

Another Athol Street operation for many years was the special Port of London Authority docks service, which was shared for much of the time between Athol Street and Clay Hall (Old Ford) garages. This was a contract service, entirely within the confines of the Royal Victoria and Royal Albert docks and operated between Custom House station and Manor Way station. Although the rundown had begun, there was still plenty of activity in the docks, and full loads were the order of the day when shifts were beginning or ending.

Also, in those far-off and relatively car-free days of the early postwar period, there was strong demand for cheap Sunday excursions to destinations such as Whipsnade Zoo, Hampton Court and (perhaps surprisingly in view of its relative infancy) London

Airport. These made use of ordinary double-deckers and Athol Street's new RTLs operated regular advertised excursion routes to Hampton Court, Burnham Beeches and London Airport for about 4s 6d ($22\frac{1}{2}$p) adult return until the 1960s.

There were various other routes worked from Athol Street over the years, but the only 'main road' working between 1950 and closure was a 1960-61 allocation on route 40, Wanstead station to Camberwell Green and Herne Hill via Upton Park, Poplar and London Bridge.

Bus services were hard hit in 1956 because of the Suez crisis with its resultant threat to fuel supplies. As fuel rationing was considered imminent, many bus services had their frequencies reduced to economise on mileage. As through services to Crystal Palace (108) and Eltham (108A) were normally interspersed with short workings to Blackheath, 'Royal Standard', it was these that were evening casualties, and consequently crews had either a much extended meal relief or finished an hour or so earlier.

Above: *An atmospheric view of the south end of the Blackwall Tunnel with Tunnel STL834 climbing the exit ramp on 16 August 1951. The narrowness of the structure and its footways is very apparent.* Alan B. Cross

As is well known, the seven-week strike in 1958 had a disastrous effect on passenger demand and was to have serious long-term repercussions on bus and trolleybus services. The immediate after-effect was the permanent withdrawal of some services and extended frequencies on many more. The vast drop in the numbers of passengers was never to be fully recaptured.

Into the 1960s

The year 1960 saw the completion of the new underpass beneath the A13 and new approach roads for the new parallel Blackwall Tunnel under construction. Diversions had been in operation for some months, with buses on the 108 and 108A bound for Bromley-by-Bow having to turn right on leaving the tunnel and travelling along the A13 to Abbot Road. This latter was the route for trolleybuses returning to Poplar depot, and led in a northeasterly direction back to the normal line of route, Brunswick Road and St Leonards Street. Other minor diversions were necessary from time to time but traffic was kept flowing, major interruptions being mainly at weekends.

Whilst mentioning Poplar trolleybuses, as their 'in service' relief point was only a short walk from Athol Street garage, many of the crews from the busy 567, 569 and 665 routes, operating between Barking and Aldgate or Bloomsbury, used the canteen facilities at the garage. This meant that bus and trolleybus crews got to know each other quite well and were on the friendliest of terms. Eighteen months before the closure of Athol Street, the trolleybuses from Poplar were withdrawn and replaced by some of the first production Routemasters in November 1959. Indirectly, the end of the trolleybuses meant the end of Athol Street, the continued existence of two bus garages so close together being an obvious target for economy.

There was nothing unusual about 9 May 1961, the last day of Athol Street's operations, but by early evening you saw familiar RTLs being ferried the short distance to Poplar former trolleybus depot via Aberfeldy Street, to join the numerous Routemasters already there. Whether there was any ceremony to mark the occasion when the last buses ran in seems doubtful, except that I remember seeing a photo in the local press of a group of bus personnel standing in front of the final one. I expect I was on my bike before that, or homeward bound on route N84 on the first westbound journey of the night . . . **CB**

CHECKPOINT

No.2: MacBraynes

Born: Glasgow, 1851 or 1879, depending on your point of view.

Why two dates?: In 1851, David Hutcheson & Company took over the West Highland shipping interests of another company, G. & J. Burns. David MacBrayne, a nephew of the Burnses, became a junior partner in the new business and took over and renamed the business after the last of the Hutchesons retired in 1879.

And he started running those wonderful red and green buses all over the Scottish Highlands?: Hold on, hold on, dear readers. How much do you know of the history of the motorbus? We're still the best part of 20 years away from the first examples breaking cover. No, MacBraynes had 20 ships serving areas where road communications were poor.

So when did the buses begin?: In 1906, the year before the founder died at the ripe old age of 93. A secondhand Milnes-Daimler was put to work between Fort William and North Ballachulish and several other services were established before the outbreak of World War 1; by 1927 there were 13 MacBraynes buses, all on the Scottish mainland.

Then what happened?: The company almost disappeared. Its ships had carried vital Royal Mail contracts since 1855, but it couldn't afford to make the investments needed in new tonnage to renew these contracts. Under government pressure, the LMS railway and the Coast Lines shipping company each bought a half share and the business was put on a firmer footing with a huge investment in modern motor ships. And motorbuses.

Why buses?: As roads were being improved, there were places where buses could provide a more cost-effective service than coastal ships, and roads were also opening up opportunities for buses to establish new trunk services. A Glasgow-Fort William route thrust through Glencoe in 1934 and a Glasgow-Campbeltown coach service replaced coastal ships in 1940. The following year found it acquiring a bus company on the island of Islay, beginning an expansion of bus operations into the Inner and Outer Hebrides.

And they were those lovely red and green machines beloved of visitors to these beautiful extremities of Britain?: Yes, but not at first. According to Stuart Bell and Arnold Richardson's recently published *The MacBraynes Book*, they were crimson with gold lining from 1928 to 1936; then they changed to apple green, lighter red and cream. They had long been embellished with The Royal Route crests to commemorate a mid-19th century journey made by Queen Victoria, then gained the Scottish lion rampant. In 1939, the company gave itself its most memorable and enduring logo in the shape of a kilted Highland warrior complete with shield and raised Claymore sword.

What happened when LMS was nationalised?: Not a lot. Its shares passed to the British Transport Commission in 1948, but Coast Lines retained its 50% interest. MacBraynes continued to buy up island bus operators, extending its operations into some exceptionally thinly-populated extremities of the nation. But it was growing into a problem.

Which was?: The deficit incurred running services, principally ships but also buses. In 1962, a 10-year agreement was struck with the government of the day for all its losses to be met by the state in return for major operational decisions requiring Scottish Office approval. This was the beginning of the end.

Why?: Because something more permanent was needed and the solution, in 1969, was to create the Scottish Transport Group primarily to contain the MacBrayne problem. It was lumped together with Caledonian Steam Packet (British Rail's Scottish shipping subsidiary) and the highly profitable Scottish Bus Group. MacBraynes buses may have been part of the Highland scene, but not for much longer.

What happened?: Between April 1970 and January 1972, the bus fleet was steadily transferred to other operators, mostly within SBG, but latterly to local operators on the Uists. Highland Omnibuses got most routes, with Alexander (Midland) and Western SMT taking the rest of what stayed with SBG. Before long, many of the peripheral island and mainland operations – previously maintained by MacBrayne managers who also had shipping responsibilities – were off-loaded on to independents.

And what was left?: The ships – merged with Caledonian Steam Packet to become Caledonian MacBrayne – kept the name alive, along with the lion rampant. And there's plenty of memories of the wonderful red and green buses.

Which were?: AECs and Leylands, mainly. According to the recent book, out of 375 buses and coaches known to have been owned by MacBraynes, 48% were Bedfords and 17% were AECs. Half had bodies by Duple or its subsidiaries and 17% were bodied by Park Royal.

Most likely to have said: MacBraynes for the Highlands. The company's slogan and the name of a 1977 book on the company from the Albion Vehicle Preservation Trust which at the time owned one of its Maudslays.

ALM

Representing the 17% of the MacBrayne fleet built by AEC and the 17% that had Park Royal bodies, two 1939 35-seat Regal coaches seen when new.

SWITZERLAND'S
BIG BUS
COMPANY

A number of British double-deckers has passed through the hands of the Swiss company, Londag. RICHARD BELLINGHAM tells the story

LONDAG is a well-established company which was originally located a few miles south of Zurich in a small village named Wadenswil (pronounced Vadensvil), however, due to the need for larger premises the company relocated to Industrie Grindel on the north side of Zurich near Kloten the International Airport early in 1996.

The proprietors, Jorg and Monika Pfiffner, originally purchased a Bristol FLF double-decker, registration number AHY 981B, for use as a mobile home during 1984 from North's, Sherburn-in Elmet. After realising the potential for operating vehicles on a commercial basis the company was formed during 1986. The name chosen as a result of using the first four letters of London combined with the Swiss equivalent of limited thus forming Londag. The vast majority of people interested in hiring double-deckers in Europe always associate them with London; it was correctly assumed therefore that Londag in the telephone directory would be quickly spotted by interested customers.

Neither partner had any previous experience in the business, Jorg having trained as a carpenter, whilst Monika was employed part time in a gymnasium in order to help fund the company; she then took a full time post as they became more successful around 1990.

Jorg obviously used his carpentry skills in renovating the vehicles; however, when it came to the mechanical side he had no experience. Fortunately, he had a friend to whom he could turn for advice. He also spent many hours reading up on mechanics and, as he says, he learned from his own mistakes of which there were a number. He is also well known as a perfectionist, a fact that I can personally vouch for, so no vehicle is operated without being virtually rebuilt internally

Below: *A line-up at the new depot – from left to right AEC Routemaster WLT 720, Bristol FLF OPU 822D, ex-Brighton, Hove & District Bristol FS RPN 10 (but carrying AHY 981B), Bristol FLFs 818 SHW and EHT 110C now repainted red.*
Londag

Above: *The superbly restored ex-Eastern National Bristol FLF, OPU 822D (re-registered with Zurich plate ZH 254044), near the original depot. Note the flattened roofline, to reduce the overall height to the permitted 4m.*
Londag

Below: *Posed for publicity with FX3 and FX4 taxis – from left to right Bristol FLFs, OPU 822D and ex-Bristol Omnibus 818 SHW, Leyland PD3/3c, RMS 677 (ex-Alexanders Midland, now sold), Bristol FLF, EHT 110C (ex-Bristol Omnibus), and AEC Regent RT, KGK 965 (now sold and reduced to a chassis only).*
Londag

whilst all running units are removed to allow the chassis to be renovated and the running units themselves are stripped and reassembled. The life expectancy after all this is in the region of 25 years, whilst the vehicles appear to be brand new.

A report in the *Zurichsee-Zeitung* in the summer of 1988 stated that the whole project was nearly abandoned due to the deplorable condition of the vehicles offered for sale and the escalating price. However, the fact that orders had been received to renovate vehicles for others' use, began to make the business viable and thus finance the purchase of more vehicles. This was a direct result of the superb results in renovation being achieved by Jorg.

Continued expansion has meant that vehicles are used far more extensively than just for weddings, birthdays and company outings. They are now used for exhibitions, information stands, fetes etc, and of course for scenic rides.

Due to Swiss regulations, unfortunately the majority of the vehicles had to be reduced to the permitted height of 4m. To give some idea of the amount of work involved – a bus costing around £4,000 during 1988 would have had a further £ 30,000 spent on it before entering revenue earning service. The cost of hiring a vehicle is in the order of £500-£1,000 per day, a not insignificant sum but needless to say salary levels in Switzerland are 2-3 times the equivalent British rate.

Open-top buses are not permitted to be operated with passengers due to the dangers of overhead wiring in the cities. This did not prevent the purchase of the remaining three ex-Southdown BH&D convertible Bristol FSs. One is operated in closed-top format displaying registration AHY 981B; the other two have been extensively rebuilt as part open-top mobile homes, one for a private individual the other for the owner's use – the front half of the upper saloon is open-top as a lounge area or sun deck whilst the rear half has the sleeping accommodation; the lower saloon has a fitted kitchen and storage areas. The stairs have been repositioned as straight rearward ascending from the centre offside and the platform is completely enclosed, albeit with a single entrance door.

During 1998 the company acquired the remaining vehicles being operated by Twerenbold Reisen (t/a Kontiki Reisen) and sold some of its existing vehicles.

Although there are a number of other operators of British buses in Switzerland, Londag is currently by far the largest and most successful operating vehicles which are a credit to their owners. **CB**

Above: **The open-top ex-Bristol Omnibus Bristol FLF, DHT 784C, acquired severely damaged from Kontiki during 1996, seen in its new format. This is now sold and being converted to a mobile home with a new roof. Its UK registration plate is just visible, although painted over.**
Londag

Below: **The lower saloon interior of 818 SHW clearly showing the bar.**
R. J. Bellingham

Vehicles which have passed through Londag's hands in order of acquisition are as follows, unless otherwise noted they were acquired direct from the UK:

Date	Type	UK Reg.	Notes
1984	Bristol FLF	AHY 981B	To Bundner-Tagblatt (Newspaper), Chur, 1990 as exhibition bus, who sold it to an Engineering School at 9470 Buchs SG, purpose unknown 1998.
1986	Bristol FLF	EEL 894C	Kundig, Zurich, then to Kontiki Reisen 1990, re-acquired 1998.
	Bristol FLF	JPW 458D	From Thermal Bad, Lostorf then sold and moved to Corsica by 1989.
1987	Bristol FLF	EHT 110C*	
1988	Bristol FLF	818 SHW*	
	Bristol FLF	OPU 822D*	
	Leyland PD3	RMS 677	From P. Wirz, to Car-touche, Geneva 1995
1989	AEC RT 2156	KGK 965	From Mariot Reisen, Geneva to M. Ghidorzi, Basel. 1991 for spares.
1990	Bristol FLF	JNU 985D	Scrapped for spares never operated 1994.
	Bristol FS	RPN 10*	
1991	Bristol FS	SPM 21*	Mobile caravan for Londag.
	Bristol FS	SPM 22	Mobile caravan for private owner, P. Hassler from 1996.
1992	AEC RM 720	WLT 720*	Exhibition unit with trailer.
1993	Bristol FLF	529 VRB*	
1994	Bristol KSW	PHN 829	Sold to a buyer in Murg-Hanner, Germany 1998, to be used for promotional events.
	AEC Regal	FVY 410	Scrapped on site as beyond restoration early 1998.
1996	Bristol FLF	DHT 784C	From Kontiki Reisen, with a damaged upper deck converted to open top. Sold to a Swiss couple during 1998, who intend replacing the roof.
1998	Bristol FLF	465 FTT	From Kontiki Reisen early 1998, sold to Stadtwerke, Gottingen Jan 1999
	Bristol FLF	EEL 894C*	From Kontiki Reisen early 1998
	Bristol FLF	KAH 461D	From Kontiki Reisen early 1998, sold to Herr Huber, Boblingen Sep 1998

*denotes vehicle in the fleet at December 1999.

Below: *Acquired from Kontiki is ex-Eastern Counties Bristol FLF, KAH 461D, carrying Zurich plate ZH 188206.* R. J. Bellingham

Above: *A closer view of ex-Bristol Omnibus Bristol FLF, 818 SHW.*
Londag

Below: *Ex-Brighton, Hove & District Bristol FS, SPM 21, at the Gardner works during 1997; it is used as a mobile home. The livery caused confusion as it was reported to be with Starlight Radio whereas it actually represents the years of birth of its owners and the fact that it can be used to sit out in the starlight.*
Londag

Above: **The roof on AEC Routemaster WLT 720 can be raised hydraulically by about 3ft.**
Londag

Below: **A contrasting view of Bristol FLF, 818 SHW, now resplendent in red and registered ZH 572731.**
R. J. Bellingham

THE WAY WE WERE

Trade advertisements for motorbuses and trolleybuses are a rich source of information and nostalgia

THERE IS always a good response from readers when we use older bus advertisements in the pages of *Classic Bus*. These adverts reveal much about the bus market at the time, as well as reminding us of the graphic styles of the period.

Colour advertising as we know it today really only came into its own after World War 2. In the 1930s there had certainly been colour adverts, but these were usually black-and-white photos that had been subsequently coloured. Geoff Lumb has provided some good examples of these, which capture liveries that have long since disappeared.

We also include some 1930s adverts from the *CB* archives, showing the vehicles and style of that time, when a confident bus industry was growing fast, and when trolleybuses were seen as the future for many cities.

In this 1939 advert, Albion promoted its four-cylinder Valkyrie, offering maximum body space. The bus shown is Alexanders no.F87, delivered in 1938 with a 39-seat Alexander body.

Adverts from CB archive

Operators choose the 4-Cylinder ALBION 'VALKYRIE'

because it has—

BY APPOINTMENT
TO THE LATE
KING GEORGE V.

—a 23 ft. 9¾ in. body space giving a seating capacity of 35/40 passengers.

—a powerful 4-cylinder petrol or oil engine with exceptional fuel economy.

—a specially designed flexible engine mounting giving "6-cylinder smoothness."

Albion

ALBION MOTORS LTD.
Scotstoun, GLASGOW, W.4.
London : - - Bank Buildings,
20 Kingsway, W.C.2.
Also at Manchester, Liverpool, Leeds,
Sheffield, Hull, Lincoln, Nottingham,
Birmingham, Norwich, Bristol,
Edinburgh and Belfast.

WITH ALBIONS—FAMILIARITY BREEDS CONTENT

Sunbeam-BTH Trolley Bus on the new Belfast route, with 68-seater body of all steel construction by F. D. Cowieson & Co. of Glasgow

SUNBEAM-BTH
ELECTRIC TROLLEY BUSES

This illustration shows one of the Sunbeam-BTH trolley buses now operating in Belfast—another important municipality which has introduced this modern form of public passenger transport. And here, as elsewhere, the Sunbeam-BTH chassis with its robust design, its quietness and smooth running qualities, is demonstrating in convincing manner the many advantages of the trolley bus. Sunbeam alone specialise exclusively in the manufacture of trolley buses.

SUNBEAM

SUNBEAM COMMERCIAL VEHICLES LTD. - WOLVERHAMPTON
THE BRITISH THOMSON - HOUSTON CO. LTD., RUGBY

The safest foundation for a Trolley Bus is a SUNBEAM-BTH Chassis

With potentially important new trolleybus systems like Belfast and Manchester opening in 1938, manufacturers were keen to show that their vehicles were being chosen. This 1938 Sunbeam advert shows Belfast no. T.14, one of two Sunbeam MS2 with Cowieson bodies. Belfast also bought AEC, Crossley, Daimler, Guy, Karrier and Leyland vehicles for its initial batch of 14 trolleybuses.

Manufacturers were proud of their trolleybus orders and deliveries. London Transport business was particularly important, and this illustration appeared in a Metro-Cammell advert, and features no.146, a 1935 AEC 664T with 70-seat body.

Colour pictures from G. Lumb collection

Wolverhampton Corporation no.264 featured in this 1938 advert. It is a Sunbeam MF2 with 54-seat Park Royal body.

The colour may not be quite right – Newcastle's trolleybuses were yellow with brown bands – but the bus is one of the 30 vehicles which formed the initial fleet. There were 10 AECs, 10 Guys and 10 Karriers, like this E6A with Metro-Cammell 59-seat body, no.25.

Southend Corporation no.125 was a 1939 AEC 661T with 56-seat Strachans body. It lasted to the end of the system, in 1954.

CROSSLEY
oil-engined chassis and metal body
The perfect combination

CROSSLEY MOTORS LTD., MANCHESTER AND LONDON
Manufacturers of Buses, Trolley Buses and Lorries

Crossley featured this 1937 Mancunian for Manchester Corporation in this 1938 ad. No.628 had English Electric-Crossley 52-seat streamline bodywork.

One of the 16 48-seater M.C.W. patented metal omnibus bodies comprising many interesting features as supplied to the Bournemouth Corporation.

BOURNEMOUTH
needed the best—the

16

new bodies recently delivered has fulfilled that need.

MCW featured a full-fronted Bournemouth Leyland Titan TD5 with 48-seat two-door (rear entrance, front exit) bodywork in this 1939 advert. Some of these buses survived for more than 20 years in Bournemouth service.

City of Oxford no.K114, a traditional-looking 1937 AEC Regent 0661 with 52-seat Park Royal body.

Northampton Corporation no.84 (BVC 268), a 1936 Daimler COG5 with 54-seat Strachans bodywork, supplied as a demonstrator.

Glasgow Corporation no.598, a 1938 AEC Regent 0661 with Weymann 56-seat body.

Morecambe & Heysham no.40, a 1936 AEC Regent 661 (petrol-engined) with Park Royal 56-seat body, complete with folding roof.

THE NEW
BEDFORD
PASSENGER CHASSIS
cuts transport costs again

MORE POWER

MORE M·P·G

LONGER LIFE

BUS and coach operators check running costs to decimal points. They have a yard-stick to measure efficiency. That is why 70% of 15-26 seater owners run Bedfords. Now, at the height of their success, Bedford passenger vehicles have been improved in frontal appearance, given a new engine which revs more slowly, has a longer life, develops more power, USES LESS PETROL. "The Book of the New Bedfords" deals interestingly with improvements common to the New Bedford chassis. Send for a copy, to Vauxhall Motors Ltd., Luton, Beds.

THE BEDFORD PASSENGER RANGE

Chassis £298

Standard Models with Duple Coachwork.

"Hendonian" Luxury Coach.
26-seater £788.
20-seater £773.
"Vista II" Sliding Panel Roof Super Luxury Coach.
25-seater £833.
20-seater £823.

The Bedford "Vista II" Super
Luxury Coach. Body by Duple.

YOU SEE THEM EVERYWHERE

Bedford quickly rose to become market leader in the small coach range, and could justifiably use the slogan 'You see them everywhere'. This 1938 advertisement features 'the new Bedford passenger chassis', actually the WTB with the new 28hp petrol engine and radiator grille. A WTB with Duple Vista II body would have cost £833 complete.

1975 IN SCOTLAND

GAVIN BOOTH looks back 25 years

THE YEAR 1975 was the last one for Corporation buses in Scotland. On 16 May, Aberdeen, Dundee and Edinburgh Corporations disappeared into Grampian, Tayside and Lothian Regions, and, as had happened in England and Wales the previous year, the opportunity was taken to introduce new fleetnames and liveries. Well, except at Lothian, where the extent of the change was the legal lettering, and the appearance of a different crest.

Two years earlier, Glasgow Corporation had passed to the new Greater Glasgow PTE, and in 1975 the new Strathclyde Regional Council became the passenger transport authority for the area, though PTE continued to use the Greater Glasgow name until 1980.

For the travelling public in Scotland's four principal cities the advent of regionalisation had a mixed impact. In Dundee, the new Tayside undertaking ditched the long-familiar green in favour of two shades of blue with white. Grampian added an orange band to the Aberdeen green/cream, and Greater Glasgow moved from the Corporation's green/yellow/white to a very different green/yellow/white scheme. Only Lothian's buses, still in traditional madder/white, continued to look as they always had.

Little difference

The change of ownership made little immediate difference to the fleets themselves, except at Tayside. GGPTE inherited a substantial fleet of around 1,300 buses. Leylands predominated – PD2 and PD3 Titans and a still-growing fleet of Atlanteans. Glasgow had nearly 700 Atlanteans when the PTE took over, and by the end of 1975 the total had reached 1,000. But there were indications of discontent with Leyland's near-monopoly of the double-deck market, and trial batches of Scania/MCW Metropolitans and Ailsas joined the fleet in 1975; the 40 Metropolitans had gone by 1982 (as had a surprising number of contemporary Atlanteans, it must be said), but the Ailsa would go on to become a significant model in the fleet, and many are still in service as this is written.

Wearing the crest of its new owners, Lothian Region Transport no.933, a 1974 Leyland Atlantean AN68/1R with 75-seat Alexander body, picks up passengers at Silverknowes in July 1975. This bus had been bought by Edinburgh Corporation, but Lothian continued the same buying policy. Note the advert for Rennies' Edinburgh-Plymouth-Exeter-Taunton express service.
All photos by Gavin Booth

Above: **Wearing the smart blue/white livery adopted by Tayside, former Dundee Corporation no.296, a 1969 Daimler Fleetline with Alexander 78-seat body, seen in September 1975.**

Below: **One of the exhibits at the Scottish Motor Show in November 1975 was Grampian no.62, the first of 20 two-door 10.3m Leyland Nationals for the fleet.**

Above: **Greater Glasgow PTE received three of the pre-production prototype Ailsas, which were unusual in having panoramic windows. GGPTE's next Ailsas, bought later in 1975, had panoramic windows but the rounded domes of contemporary Atlanteans rather than the peaks normally associated with Ailsas. No.AV3 is seen in September 1975 in St Enoch Square, Glasgow.**

Below: **Looking impressive in its short-lived yellow/cream livery, Alexanders (Northern) NPE35, one of six Leyland Leopard PSU5/4R with 42-seat Alexander M type bodies delivered in March 1975 for the Aberdeen-London services. From 1976 these coaches were repainted into blue/white corporate livery. It is seen outside the Walter Alexander coachworks at Falkirk.**

Aberdeen Corporation, after years of dual-sourcing AEC and Daimler double-deckers, started dabbling with rear-engined double-deckers from 1966 and also turned to single-deckers in a big way. As well as Atlantean and Fleetline double-deckers, it started buying AEC Swifts and Reliances, and Leyland Tiger Cubs, before moving on to Leyland Nationals in 1973. The Leyland Atlantean became Grampian's standard double-decker from 1976.

Dundee had built up a fleet of Daimler CVG6 double-deckers, and moved on to Fleetlines in 1964, but, like Aberdeen, it also dabbled in single-deckers, first AEC Reliances and Swifts, and then single-deck Fleetlines. Tayside moved very definitely to the recently-introduced Ailsa, and built up a significant fleet from 1976.

Apart from small batches of single-deckers, Edinburgh was a staunch Atlantean customer, and Lothian continued in the same tradition, with only a small batch of Leopards to add variety in 1975.

Outside the four cities, Scottish Bus Group companies provided the bulk of bus services. There were seven companies in SBG at this time: Alexanders (Fife), Alexanders (Midland), Alexanders (Northern), Central SMT, Highland Omnibuses, Scottish Omnibuses (Eastern Scottish) and Western SMT.

Workhorse

The Leyland Leopard, with Alexander Y type body, was very much SBG's workhorse, and deliveries continued in 1975, just as they had done in 1974, and 1973 . . . and would do for a number of years yet.

But there were interlopers threatening the Leopard's dominance of SBG orders. At one end of the scale were the lightweights. These had been around in the Highland and Northern fleets for some years, principally Fords in recent years, and they would spread into the Fife and Midland fleets. Both 10m long R1014s and 11m R1114s were bought, many with Alexander Y type bodies, but an increasing number with Duple Dominant bodies. When used sensibly, the Fords were useful vehicles for SBG fleets. They were more than adequate for lighter duties, but – perhaps not surprisingly – they were troublesome when they strayed on to express and tightly-timed interurban work.

The same could be said of the Bedfords that Eastern Scottish preferred. VAM5s and VAM70s, and later YRQs and YRTs, were well-suited to much of the company's Borders territory, but it was Eastern's custom to run new buses in from its New Street depot in Edinburgh, where a heavyweight bus was usually more suitable.

The Central and Western companies, wisely perhaps, chose to avoid lightweights, apart from a few coaches for Central. In 1975 both companies took deliveries of Y type Leopards. Western also received the first ever imported chassis ordered for the group – Volvo B58s with Alexander M type bodies for its Glasgow-London express services.

Below: **Alexanders (Midland) bought its first Fords in 1974, and no.MT15, an R1114 with 53-seat Alexander Y type bodywork is seen in October 1974 on an Omnibus Society Scottish Branch tour. It was allocated to the Glasgow area depot of Kirkintilloch, formerly used by Alexanders subsidiary, David Lawson Ltd.**

M types

SBG's first M type coaches had been on Bristol REMH6G chassis, but this chassis was no longer available in Britain, and the group companies turned to other suppliers. Western chose Volvo, but Eastern, Fife and Northern chose 12m Leyland Leopards for new M types delivered in 1975. These were delivered in the company's own colours – black/white for Western, yellow/black for Eastern, red/cream for Fife, yellow/cream for Northern – but these coaches only carried these colours for a short time, as the group was already working on a new corporate blue/white livery for its London coaches, and this would appear in 1976.

The other new type that was beginning to appear in SBG fleets was the Seddon Pennine VII, developed for the group as a Gardner-engined Leopard substitute. Irritated by Leyland's reluctance to fit the trusty Gardner 6HLXB in its Leopard, group engineers worked to develop the Pennine, and although the prototype had first appeared in the Eastern fleet in 1973, bulk deliveries started in 1975. Eastern took Seddons in substantial numbers from that year, and Western took Seddons as well as Leopards from 1976.

So where were the double-deckers? The group was going through one of its single-deck phases at the time. It was still suffering from the aftermath of the industrial troubles of the early 1970s which had caused chassis and body deliveries to get out of sequence, and it was unhappy about Leyland's dominance of the double-deck market and its apparent intention to steer all double-deck orders towards its B15 model, which would later go into production as the Titan. SBG was never keen on over-sophistication, and preferred the simpler – and Gardner-engined – Fleetline instead. If the truth is told, it would really have preferred to continue buying Bristol FLF Lodekkas, and managed to augment its fleet of these in 1972/3 by swapping its unhappy Bristol VRTs with National Bus Company FLFs.

New FLF

Just as SBG had conceived the Pennine VII jointly with Seddon, it was in talks with Scottish-based Volvo distributors, Ailsa Trucks, to produce what SBG hoped would be a new FLF. Ailsa, perhaps realising the limitations of this layout in the era of driver-only operation, produced a bus that combined a compact front-mounted Volvo engine in a contemporary chassis frame. So the Ailsa was born, and in 1975 the first production Ailsas were delivered to the Fife company, which received all 40 of the first order. The Ailsa would go on to be used in all SBG's fleets in Scotland's central belt.

But the Ailsa was not the only double-decker delivered to SBG that year; Eastern received Daimler Fleetlines with ECW bodywork.

Below: *The Eastern Scottish main depot at New Street, Edinburgh, used new vehicles for a time until they were passed on to other depots in the company. No.ZC729, a 1975 Bedford YRT with 49-seat dual-purpose Alexander body, is seen in use on a City Sightseeing Tour in Edinburgh's Holyrood Park when new in August. It carries the wrong registration; is should show* **MSF 729P.**

Above: **As Glasgow's new Buchanan bus station takes shape behind, four SBG double-deckers sit in the sun in September 1975. Three are from the Alexanders (Midland) fleet – no.MRB234, a 1960 Leyland Titan PD3/3 (though with St Helens-style front) with 67-seat Alexander lowbridge body; no.MRB258, a 1961 Leyland Titan PD3/3c created from older Tiger chassis and mechanical units and a new Alexander 67-seat lowbridge body; and no.MRF112, a 1971 Daimler Fleetline with ECW 77-seat body, newly acquired from Central SMT. On the right is Eastern Scottish no.AA977, a 1967 Bristol Lodekka FLF6G with 70-seat ECW body, acquired in 1973 from Eastern Counties in exchange for a Bristol VRT.**

Below: **Y types awaiting collection at the Walter Alexander coachworks at Falkirk in October 1975. On the left is Alexanders (Midland) no.MT43, a Ford R1114 53-seater. Alongside are three Lothian Leyland Leopard PSU3C/4R 53-seaters and an early production Seddon Pennine VII 49-seater for Eastern Scottish.**

Right: **Eastern Scottish received 25 Daimler Fleetlines with ECW bodywork in 1975. no.DD712 is seen when brand-new in October 1975 in St. Andrew Square, Edinburgh.**

Below: **Typical coaches of 1975 are represented in this line-up at the SMT 'fringe' coach show at its Finnieston, Glasgow, premises, held to coincide with the Scottish Motor Show at nearby Kelvin Hall. All are Bedfords of YRQ, YRT and VAS varieties, and the bodywork is by Duple, Plaxton and Willowbrook.**

Over 7,000 buses and coaches were in public ownership in Scotland in 1975. SBG companies had over 4,500, Greater Glasgow PTE 1,300, and the three regional fleets added around a further 1,200.

Fondly remembered

Then there was a substantial gap to the independent fleets. The most fondly-remembered companies were grouped in the Ayrshire and Paisley areas. The two Ayrshire co-operatives, AA and A1, had 42 and 70 vehicles respectively. Paisley still had Cunningham's (18 buses), Graham's (29 buses), McGill's (19 buses) and Paton's (27 buses). Over the years, these much-revered companies would be picked off by the major fleets.

Other sizeable independents in Scotland at the time – and the word 'sizeable' is relative when you consider the might of the public sector fleets – were well-known names like Garelochhead Coach Services (44), Hutchison of Overtown (27), McLennan of Spittalfield (40 vehicles), and Park's of Hamilton (50). Some fleets, and this included Garelochhead as well as Greyhound of Arbroath and Newton of Dingwall, had 40-plus buses mainly because of contract work.

The new regions which took control in 1975 had a greater involvement in securing and subsidising transport matters than their county predecessors, and this would lead to friction between Scottish Bus Group and the regions – and their bus-operating units in particular. This slightly uneasy situation would continue until the preparations for deregulation 10 years later – and then things got even worse . . . **CB**

Above: *The first production Ailsas were allocated to Alexanders (Fife), which received 40 in 1975. No.FRA7, with 79-seat Alexander AV bodywork, is seen against the backdrop of Dunfermline Abbey in October 1975.*

Left: *Secondhand double-deckers were popular with some of Scotland's better-known independent operators. Cunningham's of Paisley was using this former Ribble 1958 Leyland Titan PD3/4 with 72-seat Burlingham bodywork in Renfrew on the famous Renfrew Ferry-Paisley route in September 1975.*

'If only I'd . . .'

Reflections of a middle-aged bus enthusiast by MALCOLM FLYNN

IF YOU COULD turn the clock back to when you first became interested in buses, what would you have done differently? As I come to reflect on some 35 years as a bus enthusiast, a number of 'if only

I'd . . .' come to mind.

My passion for buses began following a holiday on the Isle of Sheppey in the early 1960s. Never mind the Saunders-bodied Bristol K6As, the open-topped

Left: *The author's first 35mm photograph was of London Country no.AN23 (JPL 123K), a 1972 Leyland Atlantean PDR1A/1 Special with Park Royal 72-seat body. It is seen at West Croydon bus station on 30 July 1972.*
Photos by M. H. A. Flynn, unless otherwise credited

Below: *Maidstone & District converted a number of coaches for bus duties. 394 DKK, a 1957 AEC Reliance/Harrington, found a new life with the well-known Shropshire operator, Vaggs of Knockin Heath. Alongside, at Vaggs' depot in April 1974, is an ex-Birch Bros AEC Reliance/Park Royal, WLW 42.*

An undeniably classic bus, OK Motor Services' 1958 Leyland Titan PD3/6, YUP 487, with Roe bodywork, at Evenwood in 1973.

Another Bishop Auckland area independent, Lockey's of Evenwood, operated this 1958 ex-East Kent AEC Regent V/Park Royal, PFN 858, seen at Evenwood in 1973.

Northern General's famous Wearsider, the 1964 Routemaster converted in 1972 for driver-only operation (no.2085, RCN 685), at the Sunderland District Philadelphia premises in 1973.

Douglas Corporation no.59 (HMN 690), a 1947 AEC Regent III with 56-seat Northern Counties body, at Douglas bus station in 1973.

Leyland TD7s or the solitary Bristol OT8, I vividly remember trying to build a card model of one of the magnificent new double-deckers used on the Sheerness-Leysdown service. If only I'd appreciated the old as well as the new! As for the card model, it was never completed. Dinky Toys saved the day with its 292, an Atlantean Bus in red and white with 'Corporation Transport' fleetname. (This was to be totally surpassed by EFE's superb model of M&D's no.DH491.) The rear-engined Leyland Atlantean made a huge impression on me at the time. Maidstone & District's no.DH558 has got to be one of my favourite preserved buses purely for this reason.

My first successful bus photograph was taken with my 'trusty' Brownie 127 which worked very well one or two times out of eight! It was, you guessed it, M&D Atlantean no.DH543 photographed at Sheerness bus station. Did someone say 'Brownie 127 tut, tut, tut . . .'? My attempts to capture one of the Bristols on film failed.

Curiosity grew during my teens. I acquired some Ian Allan BBFs (the 'British Bus Fleets' series for the uninitiated) and bought my first *Buses Illustrated* in October 1963. By 1965, I was a regular subscriber and have been ever since. I also bought a copy of the first *Buses Annual* for 1963. The one or two gaps I had in this collection were filled by a chance find at the original Fairbourne Railway (incidentally, the lady who served me has since become my stepmother!).

Risky and expensive

Interest in buses was restricted to spotting in London and the Home Counties. Photography was risky and far too expensive. I vividly remember searching for London Transport's XAs, standing and gazing in at the entrance to Chalk Farm's garage in the hope of a brief glimpse – not daring to venture in. These were the days of the 'Red Rover' experience. Occasionally, I would give up on buses at White City and complete the journey home by tube to Ruislip Gardens (yes, I spotted LT trains too).

Two major events occurred in 1968. First, I started teacher training in Birmingham. Second, I had a new camera for my 18th birthday – a brand new Kodak Instamatic with a choice a six weather conditions to choose from. (Is this man mad or something?) Imagine the disappointment then of receiving square prints. Today, it's even worse. All those photographs of past vehicles which are not up to the standard required for printing in *Classic Bus*.

Above: **One of London Transport's first six Leyland Nationals, LS6 (TGY 106M) of 1973, seen at Clapton Pond in January 1975.**

Left: **London Transport also bought Metro-Scanias for evaluation against the Nationals. MS5 (PGC 205L), a 1973 Scania CR111MH with Metro-Cammell body, is seen in January 1975; these buses were sold in 1976.**

Until I went to college, I was a loner as far as buses were concerned. Friends from school came train spotting. I have glorious memories of visiting locosheds in the twilight years of steam with or without permission! But buses . . . Family holidays to Kent, Sussex, Devon and Wales would see me disappear on my own on the buses. In those days you could. On 18 September 1970, during my last holiday with my parents, I went out to explore services in Pembrokeshire from Aberporth – a splendid day out on Western Welsh (from Cardigan). This took me to Fishguard, Haverfordwest, a ferry to Silcox of Pembroke Dock, Milford Haven, St David's via Haverfordwest and back to Fishguard and Cardigan. The ale in a hostelry in Fishguard was perfect, but unfortunately, only rented – the driver to Cardigan kindly stopping at a lay-by en route! Imagine my horror to learn that Western Welsh was pulling out of the area at the end of that week. I did wonder why television crews were interviewing people in the streets. The route between Aberporth and Cardigan was jointly operated by Crosville and Richards of Moylgrove. Richards are still well-established in the area and cover a number of those former Western Welsh routes today.

Exercise

Wednesday afternoons at college were devoted to buses. I preferred to walk round bus stations and garages as my source of exercise rather than playing football, rugby or cricket as was expected. Walsall was always a favourite destination – a wide variety of buses and trolleybuses (come back, all is forgiven!). At weekends, we would venture into the midland counties on the vast Midland Red network.

By the end of my first year, plans were in place for a bus holiday. This took the form of a Southern and Western National one-week ticket. Journeys were plotted in advance and bed and breakfast accommodation booked. We journeyed down to Bournemouth on no.2238, a Royal Blue ECW-bodied Bristol MW6G, on 6 September 1969. From there we travelled to Land's End on stage services. Well, almost. We were forced to take the train from Liskeard to St Austell (hauled by a 'Western' class diesel). We returned by way of the north Cornwall and Devon coast via Cambourne, Redruth, Newquay, Wadebridge, Boscastle, Bude, Bideford and Lynmouth to Taunton to catch a Royal Blue Bristol RELH6G. Two journeys were on local independents. One, the journey from Penzance to Leedstown, was on Grenville's EJY 357, a lowbridge all-Leyland Titan PD2/1 which started life with Plymouth. It would be impossible to repeat the experience today. Such have been the changes to services in the area.

All photographs on this epic tour were taken with the Instamatic – I won't dwell on this. One particular find was PRF 167. This belonged to Parson's of Holsworth and was a Bedford OB. What's strange

Top: *West Midlands PTE no.4172 (YOX 172K) of 1972, one of an early batch of MCW-bodied 76-seat Daimler Fleetlines delivered to the PTE, in Birmingham city centre in 1974.*

Above: *Kent was a favourite destination, and this photo of East Kent 1959 AEC Regent V/Park Royal PFN 880 at Canterbury in August 1968 is just to prove that you can get a reasonable print from a Brownie 127 camera.*

Ex-Eastern National 1953 ECW-bodied Bristol KSW5G, VNO 866, working for Cranham's of Whittlesea in 1972.

Western National no.1947 (VDV 781), a 1958 Bristol Lodekka LD6G with ECW body, at Weymouth in 1974.

Above: **In the short-lived Alder Valley red/white livery, ex-Aldershot & District no.854 (AAA 527C), a 1965 Dennis Loline III with 68-seat Weymann body, at Maidenhead bus station in 1973. The buses in the background are painted in the lighter NBC poppy red.**

Left: **One of Great Yarmouth Corporation's three unique 28ft-long Leyland Atlantean PDR1/2s with Roe bodywork, bought in 1966, no.55 (EEX 855D) on the seafront in 1972.**

about that? Well, this OB had a full-fronted 29-seat body by Churchill.

Morris Minor

This was the first of several bus holidays. Two visits to Wales and one to the northeast were covered by bus, East Anglia by Morris Minor (greater mileage possible, more out-of-the-way places but not so much fun). Our visit to Southend Corporation was amazing. We wrote for permission in advance and a driver was put at our disposal to shunt vehicles around for us to photograph. Another holiday was spent on the Isle of Man with time split between buses, trams, trains,

sightseeing and the beach – the price of taking a young lady along with us. Some of my best photographs were taken on this occasion including Isle of Man Road Services no.55 grounded between road and verge!

I suspect opportunities for bus holidays are improving as the powers-that-be start to realise the full potential of bus travel. The only problem now is 'she who must be obeyed' – a day or maybe two is possible. A week – forget it! If only I'd (we'd) not included a female on a bus holiday. No, that's unfair! My wife has always been supportive – she got herself on the front cover of *Buses* on one occasion alongside an ex-Eastern National FLF coach!

Notebook

This brings me to my next 'if only I'd . . .'. I did keep a travel log on my first bus holiday but just where did I put that notebook? I wish now I'd kept a record of all my bus journeys with relevant notes. I do have a record of sorts – an inventory of photographs taken – but this only serves as an 'aide memoire'. For example, photographs taken on 27 October 1973 were in Cannock, Uttoxeter, Burton on Trent, Derby and Nottingham. This was the day we went from Perry Barr in Birmingham to Nottingham by independent bus, travelling on Harper Brothers and Green Bus of Rugeley (both since taken over by Midland Red), Stevenson's of Spath, Blue Bus (taken over by Derby) and Barton. Rides included Green Bus's TBU 598G, the first Seddon Pennine RU, a vehicle we first used on 4 April 1969 on its maiden run in public service demonstrating for Halifax Corporation.

Above: *Visits to bus depots can reveal hidden treasures, perhaps no more so than at the Gotham premises of South Notts, where the fleet's history could be traced in the scrapline. Here, in October 1979, are Leylands of the Tiger, Royal Tiger, Titan and Lion LT5 variety.*

Left: *Maidstone & District no.DH222 (JKM 919), a 1948 Bristol K6A with Saunders 56-seat body, seen in Hastings. A number of similar buses were allocated to the Isle of Sheppey.*
R. H. G. Simpson

Photographically, the turning-point came in 1972 with the acquisition of my first (secondhand) 35mm camera. Quality improved but it was not consistent. The arrival of an Access card upon its launch led to a visit to Camera House in Birmingham. Not having a clue about apertures or shutter speeds I opted for a Minolta High-Matic E – another 'if only I'd . . .'. Automatic cameras then were all right for stationary objects but buses often move. It could not cope with moving vehicles. I moved on to a Practika MTL5 which was OK but I still wanted an automatic camera. The problem was finally resolved in August 1996 when I received a Pentax MZ5 as a birthday present (good old Dad!). This is a dream camera – from manual to fully automatic – brilliant for me. I am inclined to say if you cannot afford a good camera, wait until you can. No, perhaps not! I have enjoyed photographing buses especially when some photos have been published. What I should have said is, 'Decide what you want to be able to do with a camera and seek advice.' Friends of mine have picked up good quality secondhand 35mm SLR cameras for the fraction of the cost of a new camera.

My final recommendation is join a bus club. You can keep up to date with a specific operator, area or nationally – the PSV Circle and Omnibus Society come to mind here. Hopefully you will have an opportunity to meet fellow enthusiasts and participate in visits. One of the more unusual visits I made was to Metro-Cammell's Washwood Heath works in my final year at college (just down the road from college and on a Wednesday afternoon!). At this time, the company was heavily committed to building single-deckers, mainly for London Transport, but was also setting about the business of producing double-deckers to the recently introduced bus grant standard for West Midlands PTE.

Some societies also preserve buses. This might be their sole function – Midland Red no.3301 is preserved by such a band of enthusiasts. The coach came in useful for a simulated crash exercise for the Sutton Coldfield St John Ambulance Brigade Division one year. For other groups, only some members are involved in preservation. Maidstone & District's no.DH159, a Weymann-bodied Bristol K6A is an example of this and is a credit to those members of the M&D and East Kent Bus Club.

We can all reminisce and think 'if only I'd . . .'. Hindsight is a wonderful thing but we can put ideas into fellow enthusiasts' minds. I wonder if *Classic Bus* will be interested in 20 or 30 years time in the photographs I am taking now? **CB**

Top: *If only Malcolm Flynn had photographed Maidstone & District no.OT1 (FKO 225), one of the last batch of purpose-built open-toppers for the company. It is a 1939 Leyland Titan TD5 with Weymann 48-seat body.*
R. H. G. Simpson

Above: *Early Flynn family holidays mean that preserved Maidstone & District 1960 MCW-bodied Leyland Atlantean PDR1/1 no.DH558 (558 LKP) is one of the author's favourite buses. It is seen at the M&D and East Kent Bus Club's AGM in 1995.*

E CLASS IN DONEGAL

HUGH DOUGHERTY recalls the Leopards known as the E buses

Above: *CIE Leyland Leopard L2, no.E119, on the Killybegs-Strabane service at Donegal Diamond in July 1977, with buses for Sligo and Killybegs behind.*
All photos by Hugh Dougherty

Left: *No.E152 at Portnoo terminus.*

IF EVER a vehicle would be closely identified with Coras Iompair Eireann (CIE) and County Donegal Railways (CDR) operations in Donegal, it would have to be the CIE Leyland Leopard of the E class.

For the 'E buses', as they were known at Donegal garage and Stranorlar depot, really did take over from the old Great Northern Railway of Ireland Gardners on the former GNR(I) routes in Donegal, while, with the decline in CIE P class Leyland Tigers of CIE, and the early demise of the CDR's own Leyland Tiger Cubs, the E buses held a virtual monopoly of bus services in south Donegal for many years.

The E bus was not a delight to behold at first sight. Boxy, but still modern, it was turned out by CIE from its Spa Road Works in Dublin on the Leyland Leopard L2 chassis, and came in two batches, in 1962 and 1964 respectively.

Donegal got its allocation early on, with no.E121 as the regular Stranorlar-Portnoo bus, for nearly 20 years, and no.E151 making its debut in the CDR fleet as early as 1965, just one year after it left the works as a new bus.

And, in their distinctive red and ivory, very close to the CDR red and cream colours, the E buses made their mark on Donegal and on the Donegal bus scene.

Rugged and well-liked by the crews, the E buses took passengers from Sligo to Derry, from Strabane to Killybegs, and out as far west as Malinmore and Portnoo, where the regular bus lay overnight in the bus terminus, a field guarded by 'gates' made from the ends of an iron bedstead.

*Above: **No.E119 in its last years, at Stranorlar in 1983.***

The Es would run both conductor operated and one-man, after 1965, while their boots and luggage racks would be put to good use in the summer season.

Donegal garage, under the care of Joe McGarrigle, who delighted in tales of the GNR (I) Gardners, made sure that its E buses were just as well turned out as anything in pre-CIE days, and, as an individual touch, their allocation carried a stencilled 'Donegal' in gold letters, under the official, CIE cast fleetnumber plate.

The E buses also operated on the CDR's Killybegs Strabane portion of its Belfast express service, and no.E158 was the regular bus, usually driven by former railcar driver, Collins Lafferty. Fitted with coach seats, no.E158 was a firm favourite with passengers and crew alike, and, if connections were late off Ulsterbus at Strabane, she could give a good account of herself down the Finn Valley, to make sure that the Glenties and Portnoo connections were met at Ballybofey.

Taking no.E123 from Glenties to Stranorlar, as late as 1967, produced a batch of Irish-speaking passengers who boarded at Fintown, and the conductor, a student on for the summer, struggled to match his school-learned, book Gaelic with the native tongue of his passengers.

And the 6.15 from Donegal Town, to Portnoo, via Killybegs, Ardra and Glenties, would see former GNR(I) driver, Mike Meehan, pulling out all the stops to cope with hikers for the youth hostel at Ball Hill,

Top: *The clean lines of the interior of an E bus.*   Above: *No.E158 on her last legs at Stranorlar in July 1983.*

papers for Mountcharles, and, on Donegal Fair Days, when a duplicate would run out as far as Frosses, transferring longer stage passengers on to his bus for the rest of his scenic journey.

Above: **E buses on the scrapline at Stranorlar, July 1983.**

They carried everything and everyone on the E buses, in what was, although few saw it then, the last years of a truly integrated bus service in south Donegal, based on the former CDR railway and GNR(I) bus routes.

There were the films for the small town cinemas, the metal boxes plastered in CDR parcel stamps; housewives for Stranorlar, returning from a day shopping in Strabane, trying to get butter and eggs past the customs men at Lifford; pilgrims for Lough Derg; Yanks returning home to Killybegs – 'Say, folks, the driver wants to get his little old bus on up the road' – Orangemen, complete with banners from Killymard Orange Hall and big drum, heading for the walk at Rossnowlagh; and holidaymakers by the score in the summer.

The Es dealt with them all, despite the then very rough roads of Donegal, and they wove themselves into the fabric of a community which still looked to public transport for the regular timings of the rural day.

By the time they left the scene, the last surviving in service at Stranorlar until 1983, it was time to replace them with the even-more boxy products of CIE. But, by then, the CDR was long gone and the GNR was history, while many of the men who had run the buses had retired, and few, if any folk arrived in Donegal by bus anymore.

A few E buses were hired to the Lough Swilly, who squeezed some more life out of them, but, by 1989, all they had were a few rusting hulks, stripped of spares, lying in their yard at Letterkenny.

That the buses did survive the punishing rosters needed to make connections in Donegal, over indifferent roads and, often, in summer, with very heavy loads, was a tribute to Leyland, CIE bodybuilders and the CDR and CIE men who kept the E buses on the road.

There's talk, with the revival of the old CDR narrow gauge railway, thanks to the County Donegal Railway Restoration Society, of running passengers to the railhead at Ballintra, using a preserved bus.

And there's a rumour that an E bus might be available, some say, from a secret stash of vehicles kept by Bus Eireann as spare stock at a secret location in the Irish Midlands.

Let's hope that the rumour has substance. The E bus in Donegal service was a classic. No less a person than former CDR railcar driver, Mickey Lafferty, then CDR bus driver on the 6.15pm from Strabane to Killybegs, taking E154 through the Barnesmore Gap on a July evening in 1966, told me so.

'The E bus,' reflected Mickey, adjusting his CDR cap, and setting the bus down to a long, steady, second-gear climb up to Derg Bridge, 'is grand. She's almost as good as a railcar.'

That's the way I'll remember them. **CB**

CHECKPOINT

No.3: Yorkshire's railway buses

Born: 1929-31

Parents: Railways (Road Transport) Act of 1928 and two of the main line railways, the LMS and LNER.

What was it all about?: The Big Four railways had lost enormous amounts of traffic, especially short-distance urban traffic, to developing bus companies in the 1920s and wanted a slice of the action. Or, as Southern Railway chairman Sir Herbert Walker put it more bluntly: 'We aim to obtain control of all forms of transport in this country and we shall not rest until we get it.' Some already ran their own buses, but now they wanted to buy up or buy into the biggest bus operators.

So they bought into the likes of Tilling, BET and SMT: Yes, and four Yorkshire municipals.

But weren't they already in stable ownership?: Perhaps, but there was nothing to stop the railways from muscling in on this sector, too.

So what did they buy?: Shares in parts of the municipal operations in Halifax, Huddersfield, Sheffield and Todmorden. Both the LMS and LNER bought into the Halifax and Sheffield undertakings, but the Huddersfield and Todmorden arrangements were entirely with the LMS.

Can't imagine it could have been so simple for the same arrangements to have applied in each case: Indeed not. This is *Classic Bus Yearbook* after all, and we love complicated tales. Joint committees of corporation and railways were formed for all four, but after that the differences creep in. In Halifax, the routes were divided into three categories, A routes within the borough boundary, B routes into the adjacent outer suburbs and C routes running farther afield; the corporation kept the A routes to itself, the B routes passed to the joint committee and the C routes were taken over in 1932 by Hebble, an operator owned jointly by BET and the two railways.

And in the other places?: In Huddersfield, the LMS bought a half share in the corporation's motorbus undertaking, while the corporation retained the trams, replacing them first with trolleybuses and then gradually with its own motorbuses. Sheffield had a similar A, B and C arrangement to Halifax, but

the C fleet survived much longer, while in Todmorden, where the fleet was much smaller, the LMS paid £31,250 for a half-share in the undertaking and stuck its crests on the sides of the buses.

The effect of all this?: In Sheffield especially it was to lead to far less 'company' bus operation than you found in most other parts of the country. And of course there was the excitement of railway nationalisation.

How exciting?: Not very, truth be told. The railways' shares passed to British Railways and everything carried on largely as before.

Until?: Until 1968 when that year's far reaching Transport Act finally ended the anomaly of Yorkshire's railways buses.

What happened?: The railways' shareholdings passed to the National Bus Company which set up a company called Amalgamated Passenger Transport to look after them. Soon, Huddersfield bought out APT's share of its undertaking, and Sheffield did a similar deal in which it acquired control of the B fleet but the C fleet's routes (and some of its vehicles) went to various NBC companies.

The other two?: Not so simple. In 1971, Halifax first merged NBC's Hebble into its joint committee fleet, then amalgamated with Todmorden to create two operations, Halifax Corporation and Calderdale Joint Omnibus Committee. As you might expect of such an unusual form of bus operation, there was a bizarre set up at Calderdale with the buses continuing to be owned by different people – in his *British Bus Story* title for the period, Alan Townsin reminds us that NBC owned 68 of them, Halifax owned 55 and Todmorden the other 12. It was finally sorted out in 1974 when West Yorkshire PTE took over the NBC shareholdings at its formation.

What became of APT?: It later resurfaced as the name of a centralised vehicle salvage and engineering centre for NBC at Bracebridge Heath, just outside Lincoln.

ALM

In the Sheffield C fleet and wearing LNER fleetnames, a 1936 Leyland Tiger TS7c with Cravens body on the Sheffield-Gainsborough route.

J. F. Higham

GOOD AND FAITHFUL SERVANTS

PETER HAINES offers some affectionate memories of Southend's 33ft Fleetlines

ONE BRIGHT sunny day in 1971 I happened to be strolling down the seaward end of Southend High Street which was then open to traffic when an extraordinary sight hove into view having just come up Pier Hill. The apparition turned out to be Southend Transport no.357 (WJN 357J) an 80-seat, dual-door 33ft (10m) long Northern Counties-bodied Daimler CRL6-33 Fleetline. Little did I realise that this and subsequent similar vehicles would form the backbone of the Southend fleet for over 25 years.

It should be remembered that, at this time, Southend had a fleet that was a strange mix of the ultra-conservative and the bizarre. Despite the presence of some AEC Bridgemasters, Leyland

Above: New and still un-numbered in May 1971, Southend Transport WJN 357J of the first batch of 80-seat, dual-door 33ft long Northern Counties-bodied Daimler CRL6-33 Fleetlines that would form the backbone of the Southend fleet for over 25 years. It was being used in Southend High Street on driver familiarisation duties. All photos by Peter Haines

Lowlanders and ex-Glasgow Worldmasters, the fleet was mainly composed of Leyland Titans of both PD2 and PD3 varieties and some Leopard saloons. Most of the 'deckers had exposed radiators with open platforms and, indeed, the last batch of 'deckers to arrive before the Fleetlines were exposed radiator F-registered PD3s with very handsome East Lancs open platform bodies.

Above: *The 1975 batch of 33ft Fleetlines introduced to the Southend fleet a body style based on Greater Manchester standards, as well as Bolton registration numbers. No.216 (JTD 396P) is seen shortly before withdrawal in 1997.*

I had not lived in the Southend area for very long having recently moved there from London. Just as I was getting used to Southend Corporation's fleet (plus, of course, the standard Bristol/ECW offerings of Eastern National) a whole new era was about to arrive and change things for ever.

Although no.357 was on a familiarisation trip it was clear from the BMAC sign under the nearside windscreen that these buses were intended for one-man-operation, as it was then known. It was in the familiar blue/cream of Southend but, inadvertently, the roof had been painted blue instead of cream. This error remained a feature of this batch until first repaint.

The bodies were well proportioned if a little plain. There was a central staircase facing the central doorway and the seating split was 49/31 with 18 standees – not quite the magic ton! Seats were upholstered in the then standard dark blue Southend moquette and this went well with the light blue and white laminates used in the saloons. As well as being equipped for driver issued tickets they were fitted with Videmat machines of which more later. The Leyland engines were a little unusual for Fleetlines but fitted in with the predominately Leyland Southend fleet.

Piecemeal

Before any crew routes were converted, various buses appeared piecemeal throughout the system. There were already some driver-only single-deck routes such as the 23 and 23A which served Leigh-on-Sea station from Eastwood. The Worldmasters had been usual fare here but the PSU3 Leopards were beginning to move across. Peak hour extras were worked with crew-operated double-deckers and it was on these duties that the odd Fleetline started to appear.

The drivers generally seemed to like them although, in icy conditions, the lack of any manual control over the gears could cause some difficulties. They certainly introduced some creature comforts such as power steering and automatic transmission and, as most of the drivers would have at some time driven the 36ft Leopards, the length was no real problem. As the complete batch of 26 buses was delivered, heavy inroads were made into the PD2 stock and withdrawals

Above: *The neat lines of no.216 seen from the offside rear.*

took place of both the good-looking Massey examples together with the rather ugly tin-fronted lowbridge Weymann Orion examples.

The complete batch was numbered 348-73 and registered WJN 348J etc. When ready for their intended purpose they entered service on routes 4, 7 and 8 and their derivatives. The 7/8 group of routes were (and still are) very busy services but plagued by the curse of the Southend area – low railway bridges. It has to be said that, as in many other towns, the idea of pay-as-you-enter buses on busy routes was not at all popular. Likewise, the presence of doors didn't please many who were used to open platforms, but people got used to them and at least they no longer had to suffer four-across seats upstairs or risk a sore head downstairs from a close encounter with the sunken gangway.

Autumn of 1972 saw the arrival of the second batch, nos.374-85 (GHJ 374L etc). These were almost identical in appearance to the J-reg batch but had cream roofs from new and a ventilation grille in the front dome. This was a cracking batch and generally reckoned to be the best of the lot. Some went on to greater things of which more anon. Sadly, these buses meant the demise of the Bridgemasters and Worldmasters and the first Lowlander went even though the rest were converted for driver-only operation!

Industrial action

The early 1970s saw a good deal of industrial action on the railways and the extremely busy commuter services from the Southend area in to Fenchurch Street and Liverpool Street suffered to a great extent. The Fleetlines were used to provide a service to London and their large capacity was most useful. However, the Fleetlines were not the only double-deckers to join the fleet at this time. By way of something completely different, three ex-Ribble Leyland PD3s with Burlingham forward-entrance bodywork dating from 1958 came in to stock. The conventional image was going to disappear big time but that is for another story!

March 1975 saw the introduction of a 'no change' policy on Southend Transport buses. This saw all driver-only buses being fitted with fareboxes but the Videmat machines, where fitted, remained. For those unfamiliar with the Videmat, it was about the simplest machine in the world to operate; but the simple task of dropping coins into a hopper, pressing a large bright green button and taking the resultant ticket still managed to fox large numbers of the Great British Public. The ticket itself carried a reversed image of the

coins that had been inserted and thus showed up any foreign coins or other objects used to pay fares in lieu of coin of the realm. Unfortunately the machines often became jammed and after a while they started to suffer badly from the effects of vibration and gradually fell out of use.

Towards the end of 1975 the next batch arrived. These were nos.386-97 (JTD 386P etc) and were registered in Bolton because Chelmsford LVLO was unwilling to issue the matching numbers. The Northern Counties bodywork was of similar proportions and layout to those that had come before but were of a more modern style based on the Greater Manchester standards but with flat angled windscreens. It was reported at the time that these were to have had East Lancs. bodies but, due to that firm's long waiting list, the contract was transferred to Wigan. Whether or not that was true, Southend acquired some very handsome buses.

Even prior to the delivery of this batch, 10 PD3s had been hired to London Transport who had used them on route 190. I dread to think what the drivers thought of them with their manual gearboxes and lack of power steering. The ex-Ribble PD3s were dispatched to China Motor Bus, Hong Kong and the Lowlanders started their gradual decline. After the hire to LT, 10 PD3s were hired to London Country who allocated them to their Harlow garage. It was not the same 10 on hire all the time and various buses were rotated and came back to Southend from time to time for maintenance.

Reflections

As handsome as the P-reg buses were, drivers were having a great deal of trouble with reflections in the windscreens. A programme began of replacing them with curved screens which seemed to be better and the whole batch was changed over. The change in appearance was quite marked and it was a matter of opinion as to whether or not it was a change for the better.

No more Fleetlines arrived for nearly four years and in the meantime the last two lowbridge buses were withdrawn. March 1978 saw the end of nos.315/6 which had classic Massey L67R bodies and were probably the last side gangway 'deckers to see service with any UK operator of any size. Additions to the double-deck fleet were four ex-Nottingham Atlanteans with MCW bodies of somewhat weird appearance and with an equally strange seating layout. They retained Nottingham livery.

It was not until August 1979 that nos.221-30 (XTE 221V etc) made their appearance. These were thoroughly Leylandised and designated FE33ALR. They were outwardly similar to the P-reg batch as modified but had a different interior scheme that involved use of a darker blue laminate for the lower panels. This delivery saw off six more of the C-reg PD3s and all of the ex-Nottingham Atlanteans.

Open top

Early in 1980 work started on converting nos.370/3 to open top. These were given a mainly cream livery and

looked very smart indeed. The downside was that open-top PD3s nos.311-4 were withdrawn and this meant that by spring of 1980 only six PD3s were left in service and these were to last until July 1981 when no.347 (MHJ 347F) became the last out of service.

Some very special Fleetlines were to arrive in June of 1981. These were nos.231-42 (MRJ 231W etc). This batch included possibly the last Fleetline chassis to come off the production line – certainly the last 33-footers. These had the familiar NCME bodies but without the vent in the front dome and without the sliding vents in the rear upper emergency window. This was a feature that had been standard in Southend for donkey's years and without doubt improved upper-deck ventilation especially when smoking was allowed.

Having run out of PD3s, Fleetlines began to replace Fleetlines and nos.348-57/9/61/3/6 were taken out of service during the second half of 1981. Many of these were to be reinstated at the beginning of 1982 to cover London work during another ASLEF dispute on BR but were withdrawn again in the spring. In the meantime, nos.386/7 had been converted to trainers which reduced their seating capacity to H49/30D. They remained available for normal service when required.

An interesting event in June 1981 was the appearance of nos.381/2/5 having had a thorough refurbishment at the highly proficient Tickfield

Avenue works. A substantial amount of work was done on this buses which were still regarded as being the best batch of Fleetline chassis that were ever received by the operator. The livery was modified to include matt black window pillars which did not really suit the lines of the bodywork. Nonetheless the average passenger no doubt believed they were travelling on a brand-new bus provided they did not see the number plates!

The J-reg buses had an active 1982. As well as the events mentioned above, nos.364/5 were withdrawn in the spring only for nos.348-50/2-4/7/61/4-6 to be relicensed for a rail dispute in June and July. Then in September nos.348/9/53/4/61/5/6 were relicensed yet again to meet the demands of more rail problems. Nos.362/7 were then withdrawn whilst nos.353/4/61/5/6 were placed in store and no.363 cannibalised. There were further rail disruptions in November 1982 which saw various 'Js' in and out of service.

Rebodying

The year 1983 was fairly quiet on the Fleetline front although not elsewhere in the fleet! September saw the

*Above: **Five of the 1972 batch of Fleetlines were rebodied and re-registered in 1984, and carried the later style of Northern Counties bodywork, like no.251 (Q476 MEV) seen here.***

remains of no.363 going for scrap but rumours were circulating about the remaining unrefurbished L-reg buses. The plot thickened when in November, no.377 was taken in to Tickfield Avenue. Unlike no.381 and its fellows there was to be no refurbishment of the whole vehicle. Instead, the bodywork was removed and the chassis was given a thorough overhaul. In January of 1984 it was sent to Northern Counties for rebodying! In due course it was followed by nos.374-6/9 but the whole programme was a very protracted business.

The rebodied buses were not received until October 1984 and it was not until April 1985 that they were all in service – but they were worth the wait. They were of the then new all-metal style and were, again, clearly based on the current Manchester style although, of course, to the Southend standard. Manchester-style woodgrain laminates were fitted inside and there was tinted glass fitted to all windows. These were believed to be the first service buses so fitted and no doubt this was done with a view to using these vehicles as reliefs on the London coach services which were now using large numbers of coaches on a schedule that covered 22-odd hours per day. The batch was numbered 306-10 but as new registrations could not be obtained from Chelmsford LVLO they received Q registrations in a somewhat eccentric sequence, viz: Q475/6/554/3/2 MEV.

Sadly, these were to be the last of the line and, as

the 'Qs' entered service, the remaining 'Ls' were gradually withdrawn and by September all had gone – even those that had been refurbished. Since the previous September they had been gradually supplanted by DMSs that were at first hired from Ensignbus but actually purchased later on. The use of the DMSs was, of course, restricted due to their full height.

Re-engined

Developments still took place however and in mid-1986 some of the Fleetlines started to be re-engined with secondhand Gardner 6LX units which appear to have come from several Fleetlines which had been purchased for cannibalisation. This process was only ever carried out on a small number of buses and all were re-Leylandised by early 1990.

As if 33-footers were not enough, November 1986 saw the arrival of no.304 (UNH 7L) which was an ex-Northampton Fleetline SRL-36 with Willowbrook B45D bodywork. I must admit that I seldom saw this single-deck beast in service and it lasted less than a year due to a contretemps with a skip lorry which was to prove terminal.

August 1988 saw a renumbering exercise which saw nos.386-97 become nos.206-17; nos.221-42 stayed the same; nos.306-10 became nos.250/1/4/3/2; and open-toppers nos.371-3 became nos.901-3 and acquired the names *Sea Horse*, *Sea Farer* and *Sea Breeze*. November saw no.235 as the first Fleetline in the blue/white livery that had been introduced on the Routemasters that had been bought at the outbreak of the post-deregulation bus wars.

The first P-reg to go were nos.290/217 in August 1989 and they were followed before the end of the year by nos.206/7/13/4, 901-3. To replace the open-toppers, nos.210 and 215 were converted to single-door open-top as nos.904/5 early in 1990. For some reason they were also converted to semi-automatic at the same time. By this time no.211 was the only bus in the old blue/cream livery but this bus, together with nos.212 and 216 were withdrawn in August only to be reinstated later in the year with no.211 having been repainted.

Ingenuity

In August 1990, nos.231-42 were fitted with dot matrix side and rear route number displays. From the outset the use of this equipment has been sporadic and can, in all honesty, be taken as a complete waste of time. More drastic work on some of this batch started at the end of 1990 when no.242 was converted to single-door H49/33F layout. 1991 saw nos.233/5/7/8 dealt with similarly. No.238 was also converted to semi-auto using a Leyland National shift as the original gearchange lever had only three positions – forward,

Above: *No.235 (MRJ 235W), after it was converted to single-door layout. The low height further accentuated the length of these buses, and the single-door conversion adds to the sleek appearance.*

neutral and reverse. Ingenuity was always a hallmark at Southend! The other single-door conversions were also converted to semi-auto. A revised livery also came in to being at this time with the same colours but in a slightly altered layout.

By this time the fleet was in turmoil with substantial numbers of RMs, Bristol VRTs and Leyland Nationals entering service together with some new and secondhand Leyland Olympians. For the 1992 season, nos.904/5 were repainted in a new style and for some reason renumbered nos.914/5. They also became the first open-toppers to carry external advertising when they were fitted with ads for the Essex County Council Sunday Saver ticket. Also in the summer of 1992, no.212 was repainted and reinstated. Remarkably this was to be the last P-reg to survive. Otherwise things were very quiet on the Fleetline front.

An era ended in June 1993 when the company was sold to British Bus. Almost at once, nos.914/5 were sent to Crosville Wales and soon after came the sad news that the immensely resourceful Tickfield Avenue works was to close. The site was not included in the sale and remained the property of Southend Borough Council.

Routemasters soon vanished under the new regime

and eventually so did the VRTs and most of the Nationals but the Fleetlines soldiered on. Late in 1993, no.251 was damaged by fire but was repaired and returned to service. It was not until early 1996 that anything notable happened concerning the Fleetlines when no.253 was given a substantial shunt up the rear end by a dustcart. At first it was thought that it would be withdrawn but some months later no.253 was back in service.

Cannibalisation

April and May 1997 saw nos.208/11/6 taken out of service and stored for cannibalisation leaving the aforementioned no.212 as the last 'P'. Later in the year no.211 donated the front end of its upper deck to enable no.241 to be repaired after it had come off a bad second in a row with a tree. The work was carried out by Leaside Buses.

It will be seen that recent years have been somewhat uneventful as far as the Fleetlines are concerned despite the mayhem that has gone on around them. After the sale by the council, the company became part of the British Bus regime and saw no new vehicles for a long time. Southend garage became a sub depot of London & Country at one stage and when new vehicles finally did start to appear they were numbered in the L&C scheme and, of course, registered in Surrey. When British Bus was purchased by Cowie, Southend was detached from the Surrey operator and became attached to County Bus. More recently the company has been put under the wing of The Shires.

There are constant rumours concerning the withdrawal of the Fleetlines and it is unlikely that any will receive Arriva corporate livery. Nonetheless they

have all been allocated The Shires fleet numbers in the latest scheme, even 212. As well as their reliability, it is possibly because of the still extensive low height requirement that they have survived this long. Nonetheless, the survivors are still in regular front line service and are still a welcome sight at busy times because of their capacity. Certainly they do not look old fashioned compared to NBC style Olympians or even later types. Sadly, I cannot imagine that they will survive until 2001 in order to mark 30 years of the type but even so they will have contributed a vast amount to the transport of the Southend area.

They have certainly earned their keep. Since deregulation, Routemasters, VRTs, DMSs and Leyland Nationals have appeared in substantial numbers but are now gone. The Fleetlines carry on regardless. I hope that some of the type will pass in to preservation in due course. Certainly if I had the money I would love to own a 'Q' – I must keep on buying the lottery tickets!

If you have never seen a Southend Fleetline in the flesh then try to do so before it is too late. They are a unique breed and surely deserve to be remembered as 'Good and Faithful Servants'.

This article is not intended to be a definitive work, but an affectionate account of a unique type of bus that came to be synonymous with Southend. Nonetheless I have tried to be as accurate as possible and checked all my notes with Fleet News in Buses *and other sources – but, of course, all errors are mine!* **CB**

I WAS THERE

Improve on the Leyland National? Surely not!
JOHN ALDRIDGE was there to see what Northern General did

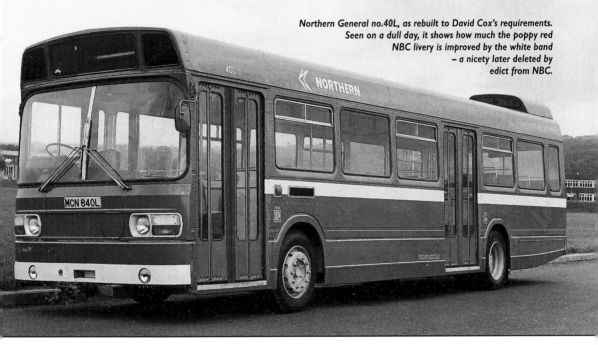

Northern General no.40L, as rebuilt to David Cox's requirements. Seen on a dull day, it shows how much the poppy red NBC livery is improved by the white band – a nicety later deleted by edict from NBC.

IF YOU work for a large organisation, or for a company that is part of a large organisation, you have to be careful about criticising anything for which those at the top apparently have a high regard. But if you also happen to be responsible within your company for that which you criticise and can in turn be criticised for its failings, then you are in modern terminology between a rock and a hard place.

One person who found himself in such a position was D. A. Cox, engineering director of the Northern Group of companies, as they then were. Northern General and one or two of its subsidiaries had taken delivery of no fewer than 55 of the first 100 Leyland Nationals built, and therefore experienced more than their fair share of teething troubles and other problems. At the same time Cox and his engineering staff were being criticised for high lost mileage figures and, no doubt, for the high engineering costs which this situation caused.

At the time Leyland seemed exceedingly slow to react to any problems and, stranger still perhaps, Northern General's parent, the National Bus Company, also appeared strangely unwilling to take up the cudgels on their behalf. Yet Cox could, along with his staff, see many simple ways in which reliability could be improved and, at the same time, the handling of the bus could also benefit.

An opportunity then arose with a Leyland National that had been badly damaged in an accident and had to be rebuilt anyway. That no doubt was important as it would have been politically incorrect to have taken a theoretically good National and spend money on altering it.

Having rebuilt the bus, one or two transport journalists who understood the delicacy of the matter were then invited to go up to Bensham Works to look at the improved bus and report on it. This they duly did, writing with enthusiasm on the results of the work, though phrasing their copy in such a way as to convey enthusiasm rather than criticism of the basic product.

All told Northern General National no.40L (later renumbered 4441) was subjected to some 33 improvements, of which the most major was to move the batteries from the rear overhang to under the cab floor. That and other alterations cut the total weight by 2cwt (100kg) and – more significant – moved 7cwt (350kg) to the front axle, a move designed to remove a certain skittishness in handling characteristics in slippery conditions.

Other major changes were larger batteries, twin fuel

tanks with a combined capacity of 52gal, mounted further forward than the previous 45gal single tank, and substitution of a more rigid (and heavier) tubed radiator for the original honeycomb design which seemed to be damaged by vibration.

The most noticeable alteration was probably the smaller roof pod, which had a revised air intake, while larger front brake chambers improved the amount of work done by the front brakes. The engine access door at the back was changed for a lighter one which also gave space for an advert, external access flaps were replaced by plain (and ugly) holes, new skirt panels of glassfibre were fitted and bumpers were removed. Various other items wore repositioned, and extra access traps were cut into the floor. Back-to-back seating was fitted over the front wheelarch.

But it was emphasised that there was no intention of altering the whole fleet in this way. Rather it was hoped to show what should (or could) be done by way of possible improvement on future models.

Only recently the general manager of a large bus company commented to me on the fact that engineers if allowed free rein sometimes did not know where to stop, and could ruin the appearance of a bus just to save a few pence. Well, it has to be said that Northern General's rebuilt National was not as attractive as the original article, assuming any National could be called attractive.

It also has to be remembered that one or two of

the alterations were by nature of a protest, the glassfibre lower panels in particular being intended to also make the point that the official replacement parts from Leyland were unnecessarily highly priced. The bus was put into service at Gateshead and in the following 18 months or so covered some 61,000 miles. By that time Leyland had adopted or was about to adopt a dozen of the ideas, the most major being the repositioning of the batteries, though Leyland did not increase their size.

Brake lining life on the rebuilt bus went from 10,000 miles on rears and unlimited life on the fronts to 20,000 on rears and 30,000 on fronts, which may not sound impressive, but actually halved the biggest area of maintenance downtime. Tyre life was probably improved by about 30 percent. The change in weight and balance also gave drivers a greater feeling of confidence when driving the bus. Lower panels went on being highly priced when bought from Leyland, with the result that by May 1976 several operators were manufacturing and selling substitute panels in glassfibre. The modified engine access door was extended throughout the Northern General fleet, though I think that registration number position

moved again, from the rear canopy to the rear waistrail in order to free up a second position for adverts.

That wasn't the end of the story, however. For when the B Series National was announced a few years later it had other features whose origins might well have come from that early modified National. The regime of D. A. Cox as chief engineer at Northern General is probably better remembered for his more revolutionary rebuilds of a Leyland Titan PD3 and a Routemaster for easier one-person operation, but the work on the National was less attention grabbing yet perhaps of more lasting significance. And I don't suppose he or his colleagues (or even technical journalists) would ever have expected Nationals to have proved so durable. Go-Ahead Northern, as it now is, still has some 50-plus National 2s in its fleet, the oldest dating from 1980. All have now gained Volvo THD100E engines, revised heating systems and other improvements. **CB**

Left: *Deletion of covers to access holes gave the bus a somewhat unfinished appearance.*

Below: *A close-up of the small air intake roof pod, which was also said to improve engine breathing.*

SILENT SIXTIES
TO SONOROUS SEVENTIES

(Exeunt Trollybi Britannici)

Thanks to the Co-op, MICHAEL DRYHURST managed to catch up with most of the remaining trolleybus systems before they met their fate

B Y THE beginning of the 1960s there were 25 trolleybus operators still within these islands, with systems in all four of the home countries – England, Ireland, Scotland and Wales; of the 25, all were municipal entities except for two, London Transport and Mexborough & Swinton, and by the end of the decade only four trolleybus systems were in operation, for all of which the death-knell had sounded.

I have always been a trolleybus fan, and still am. By 1960, I had been photographing buses for 10 years and had managed to cover most of the existing trolleybus operators but there was a few I had to 'bag' still and these were spread all over the country. However, due mainly to my work commitments I had not been able

to capture on film the trolleybuses of Darlington or Pontypridd and I was determined that this was not going to happen with those other such systems that at the time I had yet to photograph, these being Belfast, Derby, Huddersfield, Nottingham, South Shields and Teesside, and in this instance it was work commitments that actually came to my rescue and enabled me to cover these six trolleybus operators.

*Below: **Probably no need to detail the date of this shot. New in 1939, London Transport 'L3' no.1450 (FXH 450), an MCW chassisless with AEC running units, glides under the frogs outside Fulwell depot one afternoon in early May 1962 . . .***
All photos by Michael Dryhurst

Left: *The in-town terminus of the Ipswich trolleybuses was the appropriately-named Electric House. Postwar deliveries to the Suffolk operator were initially on Karrier chassis and then Sunbeam, in all cases bodied by Park Royal. This is 1950 Sunbeam F4 no.117 (ADX 187), many of which batch were sold for further service with Walsall. A feature of Ipswich trolleybuses were the unpainted and polished panels on the lower deck.*

Below: *In the mid-1930s the City of Portsmouth Passenger Transport Department converted its tram system to trolleybus operation and after trials with various types settled on the AEC 661T as its standard, followed by its postwar successor, the BUT 9611T. Seen here at The Hard terminus is no.311 (ERV 936) of 1951, fitted with Burlingham body. The Portsmouth livery was burgundy/white with grey roof.*

Above: *Judging by the lack of people on the pavement, it must have been early-closing day in South Shields as no.244 (CU 4605), a Corporation 1946 Karrier W4 with Roe austerity body, heads out of town. South Shields trolleybuses were an attractive mid blue/cream with grey roof.*

At the time I was working as an assistant director with a London company that specialised in the production of commercials and documentaries, and in 1962 that company secured a contract from the Co-operative Wholesale Society to produce the commercials for the television campaign 'Come Co-operative Shopping'. In this advertising series we were to shoot commercials in selected cities and towns, those venues that were chosen being done so (usually) because there was an impressive Co-op store thereat or a new Co-op supermarket was about to open, but before a final selection had taken place the locations had to be seen and the stores inspected, to ensure everything was cinematically acceptable, and guess who it was who suggested candidate towns and guess what mode of transport featured on the local scene . . ?

Co-operative shopping

Doug Haigh, that was his name . . . Employed by CWS Advertising in Manchester, Doug was a senior producer in its TV department and he was the gent who travelled with me the length and breadth of England and Wales looking at 'Co-ops', and he was the same gent who at the beginning of our acquaintanceship found it amusing that a fully-grown man called repeatedly for the car to be stopped so that a photograph could be taken of a bus, although within a matter of days this same man was grimacing and groaning whenever a bus, coach or trolleybus hove into view, but then, there were compensations . . .

Each individual commercial 'starred' a housewife

and it had been decided that rather than being an actress this lady would be a resident of the particular town we were highlighting, and thus had to be a shopper at, and hopefully a member of, the local Co-op. So, in addition to choosing suitable Co-op stores and supermarkets, we had now the difficult, onerous and thankless task of standing in Co-op establishments and looking out for very attractive ladies and when having spotted same we had the added hardship of having to ~~chat them up~~ engage them in conversation to see if they had that certain . . . something, and also to determine whether they were members of the Co-op, and if so, would they be interested in appearing in a television commercial, for which they would be paid. Although (as anyone who knows me would readily agree) I have never been one for the ~~birds~~ ladies, this particular chore of those location recces quickly became less odious, but certainly Doug gave it his all, but then he was an advertising man through and through and eventually we arrived at a compromise, which was in return for devoting a greater part of the time to the tedious chore of ~~bird-spotting~~ lady-interviewing, Doug would agree to go to any town I nominated in order for me to photograph the local

Above: **Manchester City Transport was noteworthy for operating the largest fleet of Crossley trolleybuses, all fitted with bodywork by the Stockport builder; although most of these trolleys were two-axled Empire models, there was also a small number of three-axle TDD64/1 Dominion buses with 66-seat bodywork bought in 1951, represented here by no.1254 (JVU 759).**

transport scene. Suddenly, he was grinning at buses again . . .

Well, the 'Come Co-operative Shopping' TV campaign enabled me to 'cop' five of the six above systems, Belfast trolleybuses being achieved for me by a cigarette, yes, an 'oily rag', a fag. This time it was cinema commercials, in colour, for a brand of cigarette that was produced and sold in Northern Ireland, and I need not elaborate further as this has been covered in an article I have written covering Ireland.

And I was really lucky to have a job that not only did I love but it took me all over the place, both at home and abroad and for which I got paid, but I am eternally grateful to the Co-op for the opportunities to photograph my 'missing' systems, because they were fading fast . . .

Two closures

In 1961 two systems closed, one municipal and one a BET subsidiary; the former was Brighton, which meant the cessation of trolleybus operations in Sussex while the abandonment by Mexborough & Swinton marked the end of company-operated trolleybuses in Britain. Additionally, the Rotherham Corporation single-decker Daimlers used on joint routes with Mexborough were withdrawn. On the one hand, 1962 was quiet in that only one British trolleybus system was forsaken that year, but on the other, momentous because the one to go was London Transport, once the largest trolleybus system in the world but within the three years and two months from March 1959 to May 1962, converted to motorbus operation in 14 stages. Yes, '62 was the 'biggy'.

In 1963 three trolleybus systems were converted, all of which had been long-term users of such vehicles. Doncaster had initiated trolleybus operation in the late 1920s and had operated a compact system, but a drawn-out conversion programme had started in the late 1950s, culminating in 1963. The end of East Anglian trolleybuses came in August of 1963 when the final Ipswich conversion took place. Again, an early convert to the type in the mid-1920s, for a period Ipswich operated only trolleybuses, motorbuses not entering service until the first conversion, which took place in 1950. The other 'trolley-casualty' that year was Portsmouth. This system had been inaugurated in 1934 and a complex of routes had been established on Portsea Island and on the mainland in the Cosham area, and again, the conversion scheme had taken place over a fairly lengthy period.

And 1964 was relatively quiet, with two abandonments. One was Hull, which despite the introduction in 1953 of the advanced 'Coronation' type Sunbeam MF2B buses still went the way of all UK trolleybus operators, and further up the East Coast the Tyneside town of South Shields bade farewell to its trolleybuses in April of that year; South Shields was one of the operators which had added to its fleet secondhand trolleybuses made redundant by earlier conversions, purchasing such vehicles from Pontypridd, and St Helens. Within recent memory there had been five trolleybus operators' twixt Humber and Tyne, but with these conversions only Teesside remained, Darlington, Hull, South Shields and West Hartlepool all having succumbed.

Rotherham had been a very early devotee of the type, its first trolleybuses entering service in 1912, and

Left: *Seen outside a Co-op while on a location recce was Newcastle no.546 (LTN 546). a 1950 Sunbeam F4 with Northern Coachbuilders bodywork, looking resplendent in the livery of yellow/cream with maroon.*

Below: *Nottingham City Transport bought BUT two-axle and three-axle forms. This 1951 AEC-built 9641T model was fitted with Brush 70-seat bodywork and no.559 (KTV 559) is seen in October 1965; the Nottingham system was abandoned the following year.*

in the late 1930s this municipality took delivery of some single-ended double-decker trams that were styled like a trolleybus. For some years the Rotherham fleet was most interesting, not only because all of its trolleybuses were single-deckers but additionally because they were built on Daimler chassis; to combat falling revenue, in 1956 a number were rebuilt with double-decker Roe bodies and it was these vehicles which lasted to the end of this Yorkshire system, in 1965.

Watershed

Within the move to replace trolleybuses in Britain with motorbuses, the year 1966 was somewhat of a watershed in that three systems closed, involving four operators. The trickle had become a flood. In this year that England won the World Cup by beating Germany in extra-time, Lancashire said farewell finally to the trolleybus when the system worked jointly by Ashton-under-Lyne and Manchester closed. Again, there had been earlier conversions, particularly by Manchester City Transport, but the relatively long Manchester to Stalybridge routes lasted until the end. The Ashton fleet was well-presented and featured modern bodywork by virtue of having had its austerity trolleys rebodied by Roe and the fleet included also some BUT 9613T buses which had locally-built bodies by Bond;

Left: *In Britain the precursors of the 36ft long psv were the BUT RETB1 single-deckers delivered to Glasgow in 1958. These Leyland-built buses were to a length of 34ft 5in and had single-door bodies by Burlingham. No. TBS20 (FYS 995) is seen on route 108, for which these buses were bought.*

Left: *The Belfast trolleybus system was a relatively large operation, with over 200 vehicles. The prewar fleet was based on the three-axle AEC 664T and apart from a small batch of austerity trolleybuses, all such vehicles delivered up to 1958 were to three-axle layout. Seen here rounding Belfast City Hall; is no.227 (OZ 7329), a BUT 9641T with Harkness bodywork.*

other Ashton buses were the locally-produced Crossley Empire, of which a number was included in the Manchester fleet, plus some three-axle Dominion models, all of these foregoing vehicles carrying Crossley bodies. Other Manchester trolleybuses were the Burlingham-bodied BUT 9613T, of which 62 with Burlingham bodies were delivered in 1956.

The immaculately-presented Newcastle trolleybuses also came off in 1966 which left Teesside as the sole northeast operator of the type; Newcastle had

Left: *The red/cream-liveried Huddersfield trolleybuses seemed always to be well presented, further enhanced by the lack of advertising carried by these buses. Seen laying-over in the town centre is no.573 (ECX 173), a 1949 Karrier MS2 rebodied by Roe.*

Left: *Typical of the postwar Reading stock, no.176 (ERD 147), a 1950 Sunbeam S7 fitted with Park Royal bodywork incorp-orating an enclosed rear platform with clover-leaf doors.*

Left: *In their livery of yellow/maroon the Bournemouth trolleybuses took on a somewhat stately air, exemplified here by no.251 (KLJ 351), a 1950 BUT 9641T with Weymann bodywork featuring Bournemouth's then-standard layout of rear entrance and forward exit with two staircases.*

operated a mixed fleet of BUT and Sunbeam trolleybuses of both two- and three-axle layout, with bodywork split between Metro-Cammell and the local builder, Northern Coachbuilders. And down in the Midlands, Nottingham completed its conversion programme; most of the postwar stock was of BUT manufacture of both models 9611T and 9641T, these latter being most impressive vehicles with their very solid-looking Brush bodywork.

With less than three months gone of 1967, the Wolverhampton system closed down and further comment by this scribe would be superfluous as the operations were well-described by Graham Sidwell in *CB6/7*; suffice to say that with this conversion and Birmingham having converted some 16 years earlier only Walsall was left of the original West Midlands trolleybus operators.

Another Midlands operator to cease trolleybus operation in 1967 was Derby Corporation, which city had been another early convert to this form of electric traction. The postwar Derby fleet contained a number of austerity trolleybuses while the standard was the Sunbeam F4 with Brush or Willowbrook bodywork while in 1960 was delivered a batch of new Sunbeams, with Roe bodywork.

Short-lived

After World War 2 only one trolleybus system opened

in Great Britain, which, apart from a brief early foray in Dundee, happened also to be the sole Scottish centre of such operation when in 1949 Glasgow Corporation introduced this type of transport and although a large fleet was built up within a very short period of time the Glasgow trolleybus system was to last but 18 years, closure coming in 1967. In addition to two- and three-axle double-deckers, Glasgow also operated purpose-built single-deckers some of which pointed the way to the legislation which permitted single-decker psvs to be built up to 36ft in length, and it is extraordinary to look back at this very modern system which closed so early with none of its up-to-date vehicles moving elsewhere, although of course by now the writing was on the wall (or certainly on the traction pole) and off the top of my head I don't recall that there were any further sales of trolleybuses, with the exception of some of the Sunbeams delivered to Reading in 1961 which were sold-on to Teesside, but it is a great shame that the Leyland-built BUT single-deckers could not be found a new home. As mentioned above, these Glasgow BUT vehicles were purpose-built single-deckers, the point being made because although single-decker trolleybuses were used by Cardiff, Darlington, Mexborough and Rotherham, these were based on double-decker chassis.

Another 1967 victim was Maidstone Corporation, which system closed in April. The postwar years had

seen a number of extensions of the 'main line' route, as late as the early 1960s into the Park Wood housing development, and to cover such extensions secondhand trolleybuses were purchased from Brighton, Llanelli and Maidstone & District (Hastings), plus the Park Royal bodies on the Maidstone austerity trolleys were replaced by new Roe bodywork, although the remnants of the initial postwar Sunbeam fleet lasted until the end. None of the Maidstone fleet saw further service anywhere else although some went into preservation including Weymann-bodied BUT 9611T no.52, which had originated with Brighton Corporation but has been preserved in Maidstone livery which is a shame, particularly as there does not exist any example of the Brighton Corporation trolleybus fleet (a Brighton, Hove & District Omnibus Co. AEC 664T is preserved), and one could say that Maidstone 52 is Taylor-made(!) for Brighton colours . . .

In 1968 three trolleybus systems were abandoned, one being the only such operation in Ireland, when the last of Belfast's once large system was converted to buses. This Irish complex was inaugurated in 1938, the initial fleet comprising of trolleybuses from several different manufacturers of which the three-axled AEC 664T was ultimately chosen as the standard. As in virtually all cases with passenger vehicles for Belfast Corporation, these buses carried bodywork by the local firm of Harkness; some two-axled Sunbeams were wartime deliveries and did not last all that long, the postwar intake showing a return to three-axled buses of BUT and Guy manufacture, again with Harkness bodies. The last trolleybus delivered to Belfast was

no.246, a two-axled 30ft Harkness-bodied Sunbeam that was to be the forerunner of a large fleet, but a change of policy dictated otherwise. The penultimate Yorkshire system was Huddersfield and this was abandoned in 1968. Another devotee of the three-axled layout, Huddersfield operated examples built by BUT, Karrier and Sunbeam and a number of earlier buses had been rebodied either by East Lancs or Roe. This system was noted for some of its routes which ran out into the foothills of the Pennines, offering spectacular views and (often) unique operating conditions.

Highbridge and lowbridge

The final conversion of 1968 was that of Reading, in November. The Berkshire county town had operated trolleybuses first in 1936 and the initial fleet featured both highbridge and lowbridge buses. Like Belfast, Reading received some austerity trolleybuses (now immortalised by Corgi Toys) that were short-lived and postwar deliveries comprised two- and three-axled buses, the former being BUT 9611T and the latter Sunbeam S7; both batches were bodied by Park Royal and were unique at the time by incorporating enclosed rear platforms with folding doors, this feature being fitted to all rear-entrance Reading vehicles from 1949 onwards. Like many other towns, there was a number of postwar trolleybus extensions which accounted for some prewar Karrier buses from Huddersfield joining the Reading fleet in 1954 and then in 1961 came the final deliveries, Sunbeam F4A with Burlingham forward-entrance bodies. These latter buses and the S7

Sunbeams comprised the final operating fleet although BUT no.144 was retained to perform the closing ceremonies before passing into preservation.

By 1969 there were left only five operating trolleybus systems in Britain; the final closures have been well documented and I feel further detail by me would be superfluous, except to say that in 1969 Bournemouth ceased trolleybus operation, this entity having put into service the last trolleybuses built in Britain and the only such vehicles on the mainland to carry reversed registrations. Between 1958 and 1962 had been built-up a fleet of MF2B Sunbeams with stylish Weymann bodies so that on abandonment some of these buses were but seven years old, but unlike Reading's 1961 Sunbeams, none saw further revenue-earning service.

Wales lost the last of its three postwar trolleybus systems when in January 1970 Cardiff completed its conversion programme.

A late starter, in 1942 Cardiff placed in service some Northern Counties-bodied AEC 664T buses and postwar deliveries were standardising on the BUT 9641T, in both double- and single-decker forms.

Innovative

The other conversion in 1970 was that of the last Midlands system when the West Midlands PTE converted the complex that had been inherited from Walsall Corporation. Under the innovative general manager, Ronald Edgley Cox, the Walsall intention had been to build a new fleet of trolleybuses based on the style of the Daimler Fleetline CRC6-36 chassis but the PTE had other ideas and they did not include trolleybuses . . .

In 1971 went Teesside and in March 1972 Bradford, at 60 years the longest-lived trolleybus system in Britain.

And so it was all over. In 1991 there was the promise of a return to trolleybus operation in Bradford under a West Yorkshire PTE programme but the necessary funding was lacking, while a little earlier South Yorkshire PTE had built its bi-modal Dennis Dominator trolleybus with test track alongside Doncaster racecourse, but the promise was never fulfilled. And at regular intervals the trolleybus surfaces as an alternative to the motorbus or tram, but almost as quickly sinks again.

And more than a quarter of a century after the Bradford abandonment, Britain is still trolleybus-less, despite a reawakened interest in electric propulsion and the resurgence of the tramway, albeit with the current politically-correct title of 'Light Rail'. But you can't get lighter rail than trolleybus overhead . . . **CB**

Top: *After World War 2 the Walsall trolleybus system expanded considerably, and was notable for operating the first 30ft two-axle double-deck buses in Britain. Less exotic is this 1950 Sunbeam F4A with Brush body, no.336 (NDH 953), the batch of ten being the mainstay of the Walsall fleet for many years.*

Above: *Bradford had last purchased new trolleybuses in 1950 and from that time all purchases were secondhand, from some 10 different operators who had all abandoned trolleybus operation, although not all entered service. In many cases these buses were rebodied, in all cases by East Lancs, some of the last rebodyings being to this impressive forward entrance design. Seen on the last day is no.845 (JWW 375), a Sunbeam F4 which started life in 1950 as a Mexborough & Swinton single-decker.*

Chassis Code Cracking

The complexities of manufacturers' chassis codes are regularly investigated and explained in *Classic Bus*. GEOFF BURROWS looks into Bristol codes

The Bristol Tramways & Carriage Co Ltd, to give it the full and correct title, began building chassis for its own use in 1908. Nevertheless from an early date they were often built for other operators, so that chassis-building was always a commercial venture in its own right.

The C series came first, eventually including the C40,

C45, C50, C60 and C65. The numbers are believed to represent the weight to be carried, measured in hundredweights. A W type, also known as the C50, was produced in 1915. The chassis known as the four-ton was introduced in 1920, with a 14ft 6in wheelbase (w/b) rather than the 13ft 0in of the C40. By 1923 this had grown to 16ft 0in in the year that the first Bristol double-deckers appeared on four ton chassis. 1923 also saw the 11ft 6in w/b two ton chassis appear, this was the first Bristol forward-control model, as were all future products. There were both 11ft 6in and 12ft 6in w/b versions.

The first 'proper' bus chassis, with a cranked frame to accommodate a lower floor, was the 16ft 0in w/b A type of 1925, suitable by the standards of the time for both single- or double-deck bodies. However, it was the B type of 1926 that became the first real challenge to other manufacturers. The four-cylinder 5.99-litre engine was Bristol's GW type, hence in later years the 'Superbus' as it became known, was often listed as type B.GW. This was followed in 1929 by the three-axle C type, and the D type which was a B type powered by a six-cylinder engine. The two C type prototypes could not find a buyer. They were later converted to E type and became trolleybuses. These were sold, but no more were built.

Below: SC4LK – Small Capacity Gardner 4LK engine – represented by a 1959 Eastern Counties example, at Norwich bus station in 1960. Gavin Booth

There was an F type designation, but this did not see production begin.

In 1931 the modern G type double-deck and J type single-deck equivalent were introduced. Both had six-cylinder engines, and a four-cylinder version of the single-decker was known as the H type. The double-decker had 16ft 0in w/b, the single-deckers 17ft 6in, and they went against the current trend by having the gearbox mounted amidships, to facilitate clutch changes. In 1933 a J type and fitted with a Gardner 5LW engine, to become the first Bristol diesel, followed soon by a G type similarly equipped. They were thus classified JO5G (J, Oil engine, five-cylinder, Gardner), and GO5G. These soon became standard, so to recognise the petrol versions these were re-classified G.JW and J.JW. There were also inevitably the GO6G and JO6G six-cylinder Gardner versions. There were in addition several experiments with other engines: J.AX which had an axial engine which was a total failure; J.MW with a 7.26-litre four-cylinder petrol engine; J.NW with a 5.99-litre version; J.O4D which had a Dennis engine; J.O6A with an AEC 7.7; and J.PW fitted with the final design of Bristol petrol engine, a four-cylinder 5.99-litre machine. Two oddities were a GO6B, this utilised an 8.4-litre six-cylinder Beardmore diesel, and GO6L was a very rare example of a Leyland 8.6-litre diesel fitted to another make of chassis.

In 1937 the G/J range was replaced by the K5G double-deck and L5G single-deck range. There were many general engineering improvements, the most obvious change was that the gearbox was now constructed as a unit with the clutch and engine. The letter O was omitted from the codes, as petrol was no longer an option. There were also L4G (Gardner 4LW) and L6G (Gardner 6LW) variations before the war halted production.

Permission was granted to Bristol by the government for the resumption of double-deck chassis manufacture in 1944. No Gardner engines were available however, so the AEC 7.7 engine was utilised, the chassis designation being K6A. Following the end of hostilities, a gradual return to normal production was made. The K range was extended to include the KS (27ft 0in long); KW (8ft 0in wide); KSW (27ft 0in long, 8ft 0in wide). Power units available were shown as 5G or 6G (Gardner 5LW or 6LW), 6A (AEC 7.7), 6B (Bristol AVW engine) and the somewhat unlikely 4G (Gardner 4LW engine).

Production of the single-deck L type resumed in 1946, this range was also expanded to meet new needs and regulations to include the LL (30ft long); LW (8ft wide); LWL (30ft long, 8ft wide); all could be supplied with the same range of engines as the K types.

In 1948 two chassis which did not progress beyond the prototype stage were shown at the Commercial Motor Show. Known as M type, they consisted of one MD6B – double-deck, Bristol engine — and one MS6B – single-deck.

Bristol joined the underfloor-engined single-decker revolution in 1950 with the LS (Light Saloon) which was a semi-integral design. All were completed with ECW bus or coach bodies, engines were the horizontal forms of the original vertical types viz: Gardner 5HLW or 6HLW, Bristol AHW, as well as Gardner 4HLW, AEC AH470 and even the Rootes diesel.

Below: **FS6G - Flat-floor Short six-cylinder Gardner engine – a 1962 Brighton, Hove & District convertible open-top FS6G in Brighton in 1970.**
Gavin Booth

From 1954 until 1961 the SC4LK (Small Capacity Gardner 4LK engine) was available for 35-seat bus or coach bodies. The LS was replaced by the MW (Medium Weight) range in 1957, the same year that the Bristol diesel engine was updated to become the 8.9-litre BVW and BHW, though the MWs were all Gardner-powered, coded 5G or 6G. Another small chassis was introduced in 1960, the SU (Small Underfloor), 24ft 4in long (SUS) for 30 seats or 28ft 0in long (SUL) for 36 seats, though a coach version of the SUL was 27ft 10in long, for 33 seats. All were powered by a four-cylinder Albion EN250 engine, hence the codes read SUL4A etc.

A full-size single-deck chassis range replaced the MW in 1963 with the RE (Rear Engine). There were two lengths, 33ft 0in (RES) and 36ft 0in (REL). There was also a high or low chassis available, suitable for stage work or express, coded H or L, thus RELL was a long low chassis. Engines could be chosen from Leyland, Gardner or Bristol – 6L, 6G or 6B.

The final single-deck design was the LH (Lightweight Horizontal engine) of 1968. This model had three lengths, 22ft 0in (LHS), 25ft 10in (LH) and 28ft 2in (LHL). The engine choice was between the Perkins P6/354 (suffix 6P) and Leyland O.400 (suffix 6L).

To return to 1949 and double-decker developments, the year that saw the prototype Lodekka take to the road, coded LDX (Low height, Double-deck, Experimental). Production began in 1953 coded LD, followed by 6B (Bristol engine) or 6G (Gardner). All LDs were 27ft 0in long; in 1957 six 30ft 0in long LLD (Long LD) chassis were built, followed in 1958 by one similar chassis but with a flat floor, coded LDL, as well as a batch of similar 27ft 0in long LDS vehicles (LD Short). Later that year a chassis suitable for forward entrance was produced, and all were recorded as F (Flat floor). The full range became FS/FL (27ft 0in and 30ft 0in rear entrance) and FSF/FLF (27ft 0in and 30ft 0in forward entrance).

Engine code suffixes remained as before, later added to by 6L Leyland O.600.

In 1966 a new experimental development chassis was built with 18ft 6in w/b intended for 36ft 0in bodywork, either single- or double-deck. The engine was on the offside behind the rear axle, longitudinally mounted. This was the N type, re-designated VR (Vertical Rear engine) before any complete chassis were bodied. The code VR was followed by S (Short wheelbase, 16ft 2in) or L (Long wheelbase, 18ft 6in) then H (High) or L (Low) chassis frame. The following year a similar new chassis range was announced, this time with the engine mounted transversely at the rear, designated VRT. This resulted in the previous VR model being re-designated VRL (Longitudinal). The VRT had wheelbase options of 16ft 2in (VRT/SL or VRT/SH) suitable for 30ft 5in long bodies, and 18ft 6in (VRT/LL or VRT/LH) suitable for 32ft 9in bodies. In the course of time the VRT chassis were improved, a Series 2 version appeared in 1970 (VRT/SL2) and Series 3 in 1974 (VRT/SL3). Until the introduction of the Series 3, the chassis codes were followed by a number 6 and a letter, designating number of cylinders and make, eg 6G (Gardner) or 6L (Leyland). When Series 3 began, a full engine description was added, eg 6LXB for Gardner, 501 or 510 for Leyland and so on. By this means engine types at the point of manufacture were easily identified, but care has to be taken when changes have been made by the operator. The last VRs were built in 1981.

The last chassis built by Bristol was designed and developed under Leyland ownership. The B45 prototype left Brislington in 1979, production began in 1981 under the name Olympian (ON); the engine code followed, T11 or LXB, then 1 or 2 for 31ft or 33ft long; lastly the driving position was R or L. The final vehicle was built in 1983, when Olympian production was moved to Workington.

One final note. A number of Bristol chassis designations included the letter X. This indicated that it was either an experimental, development or pre-production chassis. **CB**

Left; *RELL6L – Rear Engine Long (36ft) Low 6-cylinder Leyland – a 1970 Bristol Omnibus example with 44-seat two-door ECW body.*

TRANSPORT OF DELIGHT

Driving for Eynon of Trimsaran in the 1970s recalled by DAVID LLOYD

Above: **One of Eynon's part-timers – David Lloyd in 1976**
All photos by David Lloyd

STANDING on the pavement outside the bus garage on a warm Saturday morning, I listened to the approaching sound of the old Leyland PD2 as it cautiously descended the mountain road into the village street, its final appearance heralded by the bellow of its exhaust and an occasional protesting squeal from its overworked brakes. Swinging the red and cream double-decker into the bus stop, the driver stopped and leapt perilously down from the lofty halfcab. 'Dave, she's all yours boy,!' he shouted over his shoulder as he hurried into the garage to sign off. As I clambered eagerly up the footholds to the trembling steering wheel, I reflected on how fortunate I had been in finally fulfilling what had always been my boyhood ambition – to be a bus driver.

It was the summer of 1976 and the previous year I had obtained regular part-time driving duties with the old-established firm of Samuel Eynon & Sons Ltd, Bus and Coach Proprietors, Trimsaran, Carmarthenshire. Based in rural southwest Wales, Eynon's owned approximately 40 vehicles comprising some new and 'previously owned' coaches together with a wonderful selection of secondhand double- and single-deck service buses. The stage carriage vehicles were used daily to ply the picturesque countryside between Llanelli and Carmarthen; the route virtually unchanged since the late Samuel Eynon bought his first bus in 1917.

Despite my early interest in passenger transport, I had pursued a career elsewhere; but unexpectedly had an opportunity during 1975 to obtain a psv driver's licence within my regular employment as a technician in the nearby steelworks. As soon as the sought-after licence arrived (together with the traditional circular badge bearing my driver number – an accessory now regrettably obsolete) I had hurried over to Eynon's garage where I was briefly interviewed by 'Dai' Eynon

whilst we stood on the forecourt surrounded by a herd of ancient Leylands that nonetheless looked quite pristine in Eynon's livery of bright red and cream. I was then taken out for a test drive in one of their more recent acquisitions: a 1963 Leyland Leopard PSU3/3R with Plaxton Panorama C49F body (registration number TRN 733 – ex-Ribble/Standerwick no.733). There were five of this class in the fleet at the time (TRN 733/5/9/43/59) – all ex-Ribble Motor Services (or subsidiaries) and collectively known at Eynon's as the TRNs.

My brief excursion in the old Leyland must have satisfied Mr Eynon because from there on I was one of the 'regulars', subsequently staying with the firm for seven years – mostly weekend and evening work but occasionally full-time when I could take a holiday from my regular job. And at this point I would like to pay a tribute to the firm of Samuel Eynon & Sons Ltd and to the Eynon family in particular. Employees were always treated well and a strong sense of loyalty and professionalism existed throughout. Naturally, difficulties arose from time to time, but somehow the wheels were always kept turning. We drivers wouldn't

Above: **David's favourite coach – Eynon's ex-Ribble TRN 739, a 1964 Leyland Leopard PSU3/3R with Plaxton Panorama body. The author later reinstated the destination blind.**

exactly get rich on the pay we received, but we knew some routes were a bit thin and there were no Rolls-Royces parked by the offices.

Variety

So 1975 saw me rostered for ever-changing duties with a wide variety of vehicles – however, my licence restricted me to single-deckers due to the fact that I had taken my original test in an AEC Reliance. Most of Eynon's stage carriage work was undertaken by crew-operated double-deckers, so my duties mostly entailed further trips in the TRNs, sometimes Sunday School or Chapel outings to the seaside before the summer ended. Sometimes Thomas-John Eynon, knowing that I had two small children myself, used to slot me in for a trip with two unbooked seats thus

allowing me to take my children with me.

Early in 1976, it became clear that I would become more useful to Eynon's if my psv licence included double-deckers, so I made an appointment for a further driving test in Swansea. I had never driven a double-decker until the day before the test when David Eynon loaned me an old Leyland on which to practise. This was a PD2 with MCW Orion body (OCO 519 – ex-Plymouth no.119) – a spare vehicle not in current use. I took it to the nearby town of Llanelli and practised some manoeuvres around a semi-derelict industrial area. In actual fact the PD2 was much easier to drive than the 36ft coaches I had been driving as it was only 27ft long. The following morning I called at the garage to collect the same bus for the test. The fitters removed the window behind the driver's seat in order to allow the examiner to shout instructions to me, and I was away. The weather was very cold and there was snow falling. The cab heater didn't work and by the time I arrived at the Ravenhill bus garage, Swansea – the venue for the test – I was numb with cold. However, despite the weather, the test went well and I duly obtained my authorisation for driving double-deckers. This widened my scope for Saturdays as I could now take the place of a full-time stage carriage driver (many of whom wanted Saturdays off). My first service bus was the ex-Plymouth PD2 in which I had just passed my test; the cab's rear window was

Left: *Ex-Ribble Leyland PD3/4 KCK 866 with Burlingham body arrived at Trimsaran in 1975.*

Below: *Two of the Eynon's Atlanteans, ex-Glasgow SGD 635 with Alexander body and ex-Wallasey JHF 821 with Metro-Cammell body, alongside ex-Ribble PD3, KCK 866. Rear-engined double-deckers never really lived up to expectations at Eynon's and further front-engined deckers were purchased.*

now refitted. This bus had been pressed back into service due to a fault on one of the 'regular' deckers, but in the event I had it for several weeks. This was the very last open rear platform vehicle at Eynon's; the tendency by then was to purchase – where possible – PD2s or PD3s with forward entrances.

As time went on I was fortunate in sampling various types of double-decker – mostly Leyland Titans but one AEC, a vehicle dating from 1958. Formerly with the South Wales Transport Company (fleet no.504) it had a Weymann H39/32F body and was registered RCY 346. Two further ex-Ribble vehicles in use at this time were 1957 Titan PD3/4s with Burlingham H41/31F bodies (KCK 854/66) which had been numbered 1508/20 with their original owners. Despite the subsequent arrival of an ex-Wallasey Atlantean (and three others which followed from Glasgow) the front-engined Leylands continued to be the mainstay of the fleet and to give excellent service – all except one of a pair of ex-Bolton vehicles (UBN 904/7, subsequently Greater Manchester PTE nos.6671/4). UBN 907 ran well and with its semi-automatic gearbox was easier to drive than the ex-Ribble vehicles. Its sister vehicle however was a little lacking in the power department and while it managed to keep reasonable time, it just couldn't manage the full ascent of Trimsaran Mountain fully laden. Having said that, this was asking a lot of any bus, particularly as most of these old deckers were 20 years old or more (and in the north of England had operated over mainly flat terrain). It hardly seemed fair to expect them to

Top: *Leyland Leopard/Willowbrook RBX 760K was purchased new by Eynon's. It was a very fast bus and its regular driver was not to keen to part with it, especially to part-timers!*

Left: *In 1981 Eynon's purchased a number of buses from Greater Manchester PTE. These included FTF 703F, seen here, a late-model (1967) Leyland Titan PD3/4 with East Lancs body new to Ramsbottom UDC, and its 1969 sister, OTJ 334G.*

Above: *One of the ex-London RFs, AEC Regal IV/MCCW buses, MXX 489 in LT red but with Eynon's name. Unfortunately, these buses were short-lived in the fleet.*

spend the autumn of their days labouring up mountain passes in bottom gear. However, most of them managed it, but not UBN 904. Near the summit, the old Leyland would simply refuse to go any further, grinding to an undignified halt. 'Same trouble again, Dave?,' the conductor would shout from the lower deck and as I nodded, he'd turn to the passengers and politely ask them if they'd get out and walk the rest of the way to the top! Amazingly, none ever complained – not even the elderly! They'd walk up 50 yd or so to the summit, I'd restart old UBN and crawl up to the top at something less than walking pace. Once over the top, all was well, and we'd cover the last five miles into town without incident. Eventually the vehicle was taken off the road for a while and the fault cured.

Panthers

Sometimes on Saturdays if loadings were light, we'd change our decker at about six o'clock for a saloon (which is busman's terminology for a standard single-decker). For a brief period we had three ex-Lincoln City saloons – these were Leyland PSUR1/1 Panthers, EVL 550/2/3E with Roe bodies. These buses dated from 1967 and with their high seating capacity, perhaps they had been bought as a long-term replacement for

the ageing deckers. From the driver's point of view they handled superbly, a sort of sports version of the Atlantean without the top deck. They fearlessly tackled our steepest hills and sometimes we had to hold them back to avoid early running. However, they mustn't have suited because further deckers eventually came and replaced them; arrivals included two from the south of England; BUF 528/9C were ex-Brighton PD2/37s with Weymann H37/27F bodies dating from 1965. For some reason, the 'buffs' (as they became known) were much slower than their northern counterparts making it hard work to keep them running to time.

Some summer Saturdays I left the stage carriage work to another driver while I took a turn on the longer-distance work, and looking at the duty sheet one Friday night I saw that I was rostered for a Sunday School excursion to Porthcawl in TRN 739 – my favourite coach. Of all the TRN vehicles, 739 was definitely the best, and, as any bus driver will tell you,

sister vehicles of identical class are never exactly alike, especially after 14 years or so.

On this occasion I was to take TRN and join a rival coach operator for the day as they were one coach and one driver short for the trip which was so over-subscribed that it must have been for all the chapels for miles around. Now the other operator was what you might call a 'Ford and Bedford' man – no Leylands, AECs, Guys, Bristols or anything heavy. Just these lightweights, which, from the passenger's point of view looked respectable enough, but when it came to driving represented all the difference between a Jaguar and a Reliant Robin. The 'Ford and Bedford' proprietor looked askance when I arrived in my (admittedly) slightly careworn Leyland/Plaxton and I was immediately relegated to the rear. In front, the shiny blue lightweights were filling up, and I was merely taking the overflow. Finally we set off in convoy, passing through the various villages between the depot and the newly-opened M4 junction at Hendy.

Now this stretch of the M4 going east is an almost imperceptible climb – I suppose it must be about 1 in 90 or so – and once on the motorway, my Leyland was still burbling away impatiently at the rear. Well the lightweights went slower and slower as their inadequate small-capacity engines kept demanding

Above: *Ex-Barrow-in-Furness 1961 Leyland PD2/37 HEO 278 with Massey body, beside 1963 ex-Preston Leyland PD3A/1 TRN 387 with Metro-Cammell body.*

lower and lower ratios, until they were struggling along at about 30mph. Old TRN at the back was now barking angrily at this unseemly delay, and when the road behind was clear, I pulled out and passed the lot. The last I saw of them, they were a series of blue dots in my rear-view mirror, and my section of the party arrived at the seaside well ahead of the others. I must confess to a personal bias against lightweight psvs; at Eynon's we once had two Bedfords but they were disposed of fairly quickly. They were of the short-lived VAL type with twin front axles and very small wheels, although their overall length was 36ft. Despite the front axles being set back (which allowed a front overhang and hence a front entrance), unbelievably the engine – if you could call it that – was located at the front between the driver and the door. The result was that the driver sat in a sort of scruffy pit – no high commanding view – the engine lurking under an upholstered 'hood' beside him, where every tappet-clank was heard and the smell of diesel pervaded the whole front end – a nightmare of a vehicle! But wait, we haven't driven it yet – well, the least said about that, the better. Let's just say that I've seen more powerful vehicles delivering milk from door to door; no wonder the VAL had five gears – you needed to change down in a slight head-wind. Not only that, but the steering characteristics were quite indescribable – the small wheels gave it all the stability of a Tesco trolley on a frozen pond; these vehicles were, in my opinion, quite dangerous. Sometimes, when driving one of these monstrosities on an 18ft road, I'd meet one of my colleagues coming the other way in a real bus; it took a high degree of concentration to keep it steady to the left to allow both vehicles to pass with safety. They certainly were a dead loss as a psv and Eynon's were wise to get rid of them – let's hope the next owner removed the wheels and used the vehicles as henhouses.

Uniform

By now I had managed to obtain a bus driver's uniform; (most of the crews wore 'inherited' uniforms from previous employers) and mine – purchased secondhand – was ex-Eastern Scottish. The greatcoat weighed about 20lb (they must have cold winters in Eastern Scotland) so I never actually wore it as I was afraid that driving a bus dressed like a Cossack would be liable to hinder my arm movements in the cab. However, the tunic, trousers and cap were very smart and the green piping set them off nicely. Co-incidentally, the first vehicles I drove 'correctly attired' were also Scottish, being the three newly-acquired ex-Glasgow Atlanteans that had just arrived – these were

PDR1/1 vehicles SGD 610/21/35 (ex-Greater Glasgow PTE nos.LA32/43/57). Carrying Alexander H44/34F bodies, they dated from 1962 which was the year that Glasgow had finally said goodbye to its beautiful trams, so it seemed likely that these had originally been purchased as tramway replacement vehicles. They had certainly earned their keep north of the border and tended to look 'a wee bit droopy' compared with their front-engined stablemates at Eynon's. Some of them displayed notices inside which read; 'Glasgow busmen say no to closure of Partick Depot'. I sometimes wondered if their campaign had been successful, but tended to doubt it. [*It wasn't.* Ed]

The ex-Wallasey Atlantean – JHF 821 – was a comparatively early example that Eynon's had relegated to short school runs due to the temporary absence of a third gear; some of the more mechanically sensitive youngsters must have wondered why the engine note suddenly changed from a high-pitched crescendo to a low labouring throb as it reached top gear. However, this fault was now cured, so with the ex-Glasgow Atlanteans there were now four of this class to cover the same routes that the Titans had been covering for many years. Now

*Below: **The cream of the Eynon's fleet – two of the three Leyland PD2/40s with Metro-Cammell bodies that had been new to Salford Corporation in 1967. They were recertified by Eynon's in 1980 and immaculately painted in the red/white fleet colours. These two, JRJ 277/272E, were the better runners.***

although I am a great admirer of Leyland products, I have to admit that broadly speaking the Atlanteans did not give the reliability that the firm had come to expect from their more traditional predecessors. The location of the door on the driver's immediate left did, of course, relieve the conductor of bell-duty (and the Atlantean could be one-man-operated during quieter periods) but all in all they tended to be less tolerant of the long arduous gradients of the area and many a cloud of steam was seen as they tackled the long haul up Trimsaran Mountain.

Elegant

Talking about clouds of steam brings me to the ex-London Transport RFs. We acquired three of these which dated from 1952 – registered MLL 934/8 and MXX 489. Very handsome they were too, with their elegant B39F bodies. At the time, they were the oldest vehicles in the fleet but unfortunately well past their prime as far as the cooling system was concerned. Any lengthy run resulted in serious overheating problems, and I suppose that this was one of the reasons that they had been withdrawn by LT. Like all AECs, they were absolutely beautiful to drive but being only 7ft 6in wide were a bit cramped in the cab – having long arms I used to find that negotiating tight corners often caused bruised elbows from the cab windows! But in many ways they would have been absolutely ideal on some of our more far-flung rural routes where the roads were particularly narrow – with the standard width bus it was quite impossible for two of them to pass on some of the roads.

The Atlanteans were eventually replaced by three ex-Salford City Transport Leyland Titan PD2/40s – JRJ 261/72/7E with MCW H37/27F bodies and very traditional exposed radiators. Unlike the Atlanteans, these Titans had gone straight into the paint-shop for the full Eynon treatment. And when they finally

emerged, did they look magnificent! The red and cream livery really did something for a halfcab decker and I was keen to try them. I soon found that my favourite was JRJ 272E and generally managed to secure this one as my colleague Ivor preferred 277E. We both acknowledged that 261E did not run quite so well. Sometimes we'd both be on the same all-day Llanelli-Carmarthen service (about 20 miles each way) and because of our timetable we were scheduled to pass each other at the halfway point on a small bridge. Ivor was, like me, a keen timekeeper and invariably all day we'd pass each other within yards of the centre of the bridge; the two crews waving to each other and the two buses gleaming in the summer sun. Halcyon days!

Alternative

As time went on, the TRNs had, one by one, run their last mile; nos. 735 and 743 had long been cannibalised for spares while no. 733 suffered the indignity of being stripped of its seats and ending up as a cleaner's 'shed' in a corner of the adjacent field where the older buses were parked in the open, mildew creeping up the panels of the once-elegant Plaxton coachwork. Nos.739 and 759 bravely soldiered on till the early 1980s when they, too, reached the end of the road. However, my own days at Eynon's were now drawing to a close – a move which had been prompted by changes which had been taking place in my main employment – changes from which I felt compelled to seek an alternative. How much I would have welcomed a full-time position with my old friends at Eynon's but considerations of full-time remuneration and of a comparable company pension scheme forced me to look further afield – to the National Bus Company in fact. The reasons for this were well understood by the Eynon family and I was assured by them of an offer of future re-employment should circumstances ever change. So in April 1982 I said my farewells and departed for a new career driving Leyland Nationals, more Leopards, an occasional 'Rapide' vehicle and Bristol VRs. Perhaps some day I'll write about it.

So what did those years 1975-1982 mean to me as a part-time bus and coach driver? Well obviously the chance for an enthusiast to actually become involved in such an interesting fleet was an opportunity I was very fortunate to have had. The years spent driving the wonderful assortment of buses and coaches are always looked back on with much pleasure, although I must say it wasn't always a bed of roses! I'll never forget the comradeship of the other employees who were always willing to help each other out in times of difficulty, and above all to keep the fleet running to schedule; the highly professional but very approachable manner of the Eynon family – always a friendly atmosphere at the garage – a company truly at ease with itself. I had been fortunate to have operated what must have been amongst Britain's last crew-operated halfcab double-deckers – and through beautiful countryside with no major cities and consequently no major traffic problems. My conductor and I always took a pride in a job well done – always endeavouring to keep to time without recourse to hurrying the passengers along (on his part) or severe use of brakes and clutch (on mine). I remember stopping early morning buses on remote country lanes while the passengers went gathering mushrooms in a nearby field; driving an old PD2 on the narrow lane through Stradey woods at night – the swooping owls and bats fleeing from the illuminated monster that reflected its two decks into the trees. I sometimes recall thundering along the valley floor in a well-tuned TRN with the roar of the exhaust echoing from the terrace of cottages that clung precariously to the mountainside. Sometimes setting off for England (80 miles away) with a full complement of passengers who would appreciate the effort that I always put in to make their trip enjoyable; and how rewarding to be told on return 'Thank you driver for a safe journey'.

Some years later, in 1987, Eynon's celebrated its 70th anniversary and the following year the firm was absorbed by the larger company of Davies Bros (Pencader) Ltd, and, sad to relate, the name Samuel Eynon & Sons eventually disappeared from the fleet. Eynon's garage became a Davies Bros depot, although all existing staff remained. I was sad to see the old name go, but Davies Bros was a well-respected firm – founded in Pencader (about 20 miles away) in 1926. It operated a very smart fleet of quality coaches (no lightweights!) and it seemed that the legacy of Samuel Eynon was destined to continue at Trimsaran albeit under another name. But, as events turned out, not for long. Less than a decade later, Davies Bros surprisingly sold out its stage carriage interests to FirstBus and transferred all its private hire work to Carmarthen. Eynon's former headquarters at Trimsaran thus fell into disuse and today the old premises stand only as a reminder of their many years as the centre of operations for a family-run company. Nearby stands Samuel Eynon's original house adjoining the 'Bryn Villa Garage' from where it all began in 1917 with a solid-tyred Fiat.

So there we are. The years 1987-8 saw the break-up of Eynon's and, as the reader may recall, the dismantling of the National Bus Company.

But that's another story. **CB**

An illustration prepared by David Lloyd to illustrate a poem about halfcab double-deckers that appeared in the magazine Coaching Journal *in 1980.*

BEDFORD SB

GEOFF BURROWS describes a once-familiar single-deck chassis

WHEN THE 1950 Commercial Motor Show opened at Earls Court in September 1950, one of the stars was the new 'Big Bedford' seven-ton range of tracks. Complementing this, and using mostly the same components including the large bulbous scuttle panel, was the new SB bus and coach chassis. In announcing this the makers, Vauxhall Motors, said that it was to replace the famous OB chassis, of which over 12,700 had been produced.

At the time the OB with its 29-seat coach body was the mainstay of the majority of small coach operators in the British Isles. Many expressed the opinion that the new SB coach with its 33-seat Duple body was just too big for their sphere of operations. Difficulties with small depots and narrow roads were quoted, and some threatened to boycott Bedford altogether. There were after all plenty of alternative chassis available, albeit most of them for lorries.

Nevertheless, Vauxhall withdrew the OB, and went ahead with production of the new chassis in plenty of time for the 1951 coach season. It had full forward control, designed for full-fronted bodywork on the 17ft 2in wheelbase chassis. The new six-cylinder 4.9-litre petrol engine produced 110bhp @ 3,200rpm. Transmission was through a new synchromesh gearbox (except on first), and hypoid rear axle, and brakes were vacuum servo hydraulic.

Duple Motor Bodies Ltd produced a new curved waistrail design for the new chassis, its distinctive shape complementing the rather obtrusive front scuttle design. This scuttle shape was to remain familiar on the S series of trucks for many years, but it was never a very happy arrangement on the front of a coach, and even less so on the rather straightforward bus bodies which were designed for the chassis. With 33 seats and a small boot, the 27ft 6in-long Bedford Duple Vega coach turned out to be an ideal vehicle for the popular party hire and day excursion market.

It may seem strange today, but in 1950 many operators were unconvinced about the merits of diesel engines; and many arguments ensued, and road tests were laid on to try to convince the sceptics. This was the reason for the introduction of the SB as a petrol-engined chassis, but Vauxhall was aware of the possibilities and in 1953 offered a diesel-engined version as an alternative. The models were re-classified SBG (petrol, or gasoline according to the American owners), and SBO, for the oil engine, in this case the Perkins R6.

Above: *The Big Bedford SB as it was first seen at the 1950 Commercial Show, with 33-seat Duple Vega body. The lettering on the side reads: 'The new Big Bedford-Duple metal-framed 33-seater Vega coach. Price £2,190 painted in operator's colours'.*

Pleasing design

In the same year it was decided to abandon the S type front scuttle and leave the design and construction of the front end to the coachbuilder. Duple produced a pleasing design with an oval-shaped grille with a polished chrome surround. This was changed in 1955 to a new profile which incorporated the Bedford badge at the top. This coincided with the adoption of a new 18ft wheelbase to enable a 30ft body to be fitted, capable of carrying 41 passengers.

During this period it suddenly became quite difficult to identify coaches 'on sight', because the Duple Vega, and Super Vega bodies designed for the Bedford sat quite happily on a wide range of front-engined chassis. Since underfloor-engined vehicles were now the standard 'heavyweight' design, many operators had their AEC Regal, Leyland Tiger and Daimler CV chassis rebodied with Super Vegas.

Many other coachbuilders had now got into the act, of course. The Plaxton Venturer, Burlingham Seagull and Yeates Riviera were joined by designs from Whitson, Strachans, Gurney Nutting, Harrington, Trans-United and several others. Even MCW came up with a version, the Amethyst.

There were also many bus versions produced, but comparatively few went into stage carriage service. Most went to private owners such as oil refineries, steelworks, building companies and shipping operators; education authorities and the newly emerging airport authorities quickly found uses for them. In addition to some of the coachbuilders already mentioned, bus bodies were built for the SB by Marshalls of Cambridge, Nudd Bros & Lockyer [which was to become Duple ([Midland]), Wadhams and Willowbrook.

Established feature

By 1959 the SB was an established feature of the coach scene, there were few small operators who did not own at least one. Vauxhall was determined to retain the initiative by updating the power available for both the trucks and buses. The SBG/SBO categories were replaced by a range of more powerful options using a new Bedford diesel engine of 4.59 litres in the SB1, and a petrol equivalent of the same capacity in the SB3. Eventually the range included the SB5 with Bedford 5.049 diesel engine, the 350cu in Leyland diesel powered the SB8, and the SB13 was fitted with the Leyland 370cu in engine. All were available in 7ft 6in or 8ft wide versions, and from 1962 the diesel-engined versions had air hydraulic brakes.

When the first British Coach Rally was held at Clacton in 1955, no fewer than 20 Bedford SBs were entered. The nearest competitor was the AEC Reliance, with 17 entries. There was only one SBO, the remainder being petrol engined SB or SBG models. Bodies ranged from Duple Vega and Super Vega

Above: *Like the OB before it, the SB found a niche as a rural bus. This early SB/Duple Vega of Atkinson of Morebattle is seen in the 1960s on its regular journey between Kelso and Hownam in the Scottish Borders.*
R. L. Iles

seating between 28-38, to a magnificent Strachans Everest seating only 27, luxuriously fitted out for continental touring.

Ten years later at Brighton, the annual British Coach Rally fielded 36 Bedfords from the now wider range of chassis, but even so there were still 13 SBs on display, all 41-seaters. This time there were Duple Super Vega and Bella Vega bodies, as well as a Duple (Northern) Firefly, a Harrington Crusader and two Plaxton Embassy versions.

Interestingly, the SB now had a direct competitor in the form of the Thames Trader, of which there were 11 entries. Ford was also competing with the Bedford's innovative three-axle/twin-steer VAL, using the two-axle Thames 36 model. The Bedford models outlasted the Fords, but it was a close run thing and it was the

shrinking market that really brought them to an end, combined with the growth of the motorway network and the move towards heavier-weight coaches more capable of sustaining high speeds.

Several of the magazines covering road transport carried out road tests on the SB, some of them several times over the years. All found the Bedfords to be good performers, if on the noisy side, with quite good fuel economy. I haven't quoted any figures here, as some results are contradictory, and some are much too good to

DIESEL OR PETROL?

You get more out of

BEDFORD

be true! All seemed to agree on a top speed of 60mph, which is up with the best of all others at the time.

Although I have stressed that the SB was primarily the little man's coach, some of the larger operators did try them from time to time. One of the earliest was Southern Vectis, which used them as a natural replacement for its fleet of OBs. Twelve were put into service between 1951 and 1955, all with Duple coach bodies seating either 33, 38 or 41. Alexanders put a fleet of 11 Burlingham-bodied examples on the road in 1953; they were not withdrawn until 1966.

An altogether more interesting example was Eastern Counties. In 1954 it bought no fewer than 18 fitted with Gardner 4LK engines and Duple C37F bodies. Eastern Counties, with its flat operating terrain had carried out similar exercises in the past with Dennis and Beadle vehicles. It was probably due in part to this order that Bristol developed the SC and SU models.

Municipal SBs

There was even a number of municipal operators of SBs. Edinburgh Corporation shared the Southern Vectis enthusiasm for OBs and their replacements. A fleet of 12 SB5/Duple C41F went into service in

1963/64 and lasted nearly 10 years. Coventry bought three in the same period, mainly for school and private hire work. Walsall had bought six SBOs in 1956 with Willowbrook bus bodies. When Cleveland bought Saltburn Motor Services, it found 13 SB1, SB3 and SB5 amongst its newly-acquired fleet. With Plaxton and Duple coach bodies, they were not all amongst the first vehicles to be withdrawn.

The BET group got a taste of them too from time to time. Hebble bought three in 1956, North Western took eight in 1961 and the Northern General group bought 12 in 1963, all for coaching duties with NGT (eight), Tynemouth (two) and Sunderland District (two).

Overseas the Bedford SB was badly-placed to compete directly with the American parent company's products, but several hundred went to work with British-owned businesses around the world. Closer to home, in Ireland, CIE built up a fleet of 50 with Van Hool/McArdle bus bodies for school work. The Ulster Transport Authority bought a batch of 41-seat coaches in 1965 for an interesting use. All were painted in different colour schemes and allocated to hotels which were involved in UTA inclusive holiday tours. UTA also operated a fleet of 49-seat SB buses. Guernsey Railways bought 10 with Wadham Stringer bus bodies, and Malta became home to many, some of which still survive today – or parts of them do, at least!

By 1970 the SB had been developed just as far as it could. In its 20 years existence the power units, brakes, springing and several other features had gradually been improved to the limits of practicability. Furthermore, its range of seating was now overlapped by other Bedford models, the VAS and the VAM. So Vauxhall announced that the SB would be deleted when current orders were completed.

MoD

The company reckoned without the Ministry of Defence. Since the days of World War 2, the MoD (and its predecessors) had been one of Bedford's best customers. First there was the OWB, which just about met most of its passenger transport needs, though it was a little small. However its replacement, the SB, was absolutely right for the MoD. Large capacity when needed, dual-purpose as an ambulance/bus for the battlefield, or even luxury seating for moving top brass around. All these versions were around, on these tough, basic, simple-to-maintain chassis. Though all the other Bedford truck and bus chassis were tried from time to time, the MoD always came back to the SB for passenger carrying.

Many manufacturers built the MoD bodies over the years, including Duple, Roe, SMT, Mulliners and Marshalls, but it was Strachans which built the lion's share. At first it used the Bedford scuttle, but it soon adopted its own – it was squarer if no less ugly. Painted deep bronze green for the army, aircraft grey for the air force, and navy blue and white for guess who, they could be found all over the world in right-hand or left-hand drive. The army always used petrol engines, while the navy preferred diesel.

The MoD acted as agents for other government departments and often bought SBs for use other than with the armed forces. Probably the longest SBs to be built were ordered this way, they were 32ft long and 8ft 6in wide with dual doors and wooden-slatted seats for 50 passengers.

Now the MoD didn't want VASs or VALs or Reliances or even Guy Victories, though they could all be found in military use in penny numbers, for reasons best known to themselves. Thus the SB soldiered on, so to speak, until 1986 when not only the SB but the Bedford name came to an end.

The continuing success of the SB was mainly due to its rugged simplicity at a price that could be afforded by its potential customers. Though it was gradually improved, the basic concept of a straightforward easily-maintained machine was never lost. When it was introduced in 1950, the chassis cost £690; 15 years later they could still be bought for less than double that.

Now it looks as though the SB has been re-invented. The concept of the Mercedes-Benz Vario and the Optare MetroRider look very like an up-to-date version of the Bedford. But will either of them equal the 36-year production run, or 50,000 sales of the SB? **CB**

Right: *An early 'big fleet' user of the new Bella Vega body on Bedford SB was Edinburgh Corporation, which in 1963/4 bought 12 SB5 41-seaters. No.221 (221 FS) of 1964 is seen at the Palace of Holyroodhouse, Edinburgh, when new in ECT's white/black coach livery.*
Gavin Booth

Right: *This plain but well-proportioned bus body was built by Duple on Bedford SB chassis for a number of years. This example, seen operating for Arran Coaches, was new to Mitchell of Stornoway.*

Previous page: *Duple continuously upgraded its Super Vega body for SB chassis. This was the ultimate version, introduced in 1961, with one-piece windscreen. From 1963 the Bella range replaced the Super Vega.*

CHECKPOINT

No.4: Southampton Corporation Transport

Born: 30 June 1898

What happened then?: The Southampton Tramway Company, running horse trams since 5 May 1879, was taken over. The corporation had already acquired Southampton's electricity generating and supply company and was keen to electrify the tramways. The process began in January 1900 and was completed the following year.

And the first buses?: Around the same time. Information is a bit sketchy, but back in 1963, in an Ian Allan *British Bus Fleets* volume for the area, David Kaye said they lasted for four months from August 1901 and that they ran from the town centre to Northam. The city council's own history in 1979 said they were rejected as unreliable, although it's also noteworthy that the bus trial seems to have occurred when the electrification programme was disrupting the tram service and there may have been a human factor.

Which was?: The tramway manager resigned at the beginning of 1901; two potential replacements were appointed and then rejected by the corporation, leaving first the traffic manager and later the borough electric engineer to run the undertaking along with their other onerous duties. A full-time manager wasn't appointed until 1913 and it wasn't until his successor arrived two years later that buses came back into vogue.

And who was this great man?: W. Tuke Robson. He came from South Shields with experience of running Edison battery electric buses. He imported a similar tower wagon from America in 1916, but shortly before ill health drove him out of his job, he bought a secondhand Lancia car and had it fitted with an 11-seat bus body built in the tramcar workshops.

This was the first 'modern' motorbus for Southampton?: Probably not as we would know it. It was used more for staff transport, to attend breakdowns and to carry dignitaries to public events. But new manager James Dobson brought experience of petrol buses in Dartford and this time the corporation did catch the bus. Six Thornycroft Js, with open-top double-deck bodies also built by the corporation, launched the route to St James's Road in 1919.

An instant success?: Up to a point, Lord Copper, up to a point. They lost £795 in their first year, prompting the withdrawal of some routes and a decision to buy smaller, lighter and presumably cheaper single-deckers with in-house bodywork. Double-deck operation restarted in 1929 with six English Electric-bodied Thornycrofts. This was enough to tip the balance in favour of buses and despite the arrival of new trams in 1929/30, buses began to take their place in 1936 and the final tram ran on the last day of 1949.

What sort of buses were bought?: Thornycroft enjoyed continuing, if diminishing support as its factory was in Basingstoke and some of its chassis castings came from Southampton, but AECs and Leylands found greater favour and later the operator became one of the most loyal buyers of the prewar Guy Arab, taking 11 at a time when most operators ignored this model.

And after World War 2?: An extraordinary vote of faith in the Arab III. No fewer than 185, with Park Royal bodies, arrived between 1946 and 1954, creating one of the most standardised fleets in the country, even if this also stored up an age profile problem for the future. In 1952-55, 12 Park Royal-bodied Arab UF standee single-deckers replaced prewar single-deckers and were followed by a trio of Alexander-bodied Albion Nimbuses. The Guys were the parting legacy of Percival Baker, the general manager who retired in 1954 after 31 years in the post.

How was the awful age profile sorted out?: Gradually and not with Guys. A Wulfrunian demonstrator did operate in the city in 1960, but this advanced model wasn't doing its troubled manufacturer many favours. So starting in April 1961, a mix of Park Royal-bodied Leyland PD2s and AEC Regent Vs came into the fleet, with Regents being bought for longer and latterly with East Lancs bodies. The rear-engined age dawned in 1968 with the first of 10 AEC Swifts bodied locally by Strachans to a design similar to London's first Red Arrows. They were followed by East Lancs-bodied Atlanteans which remained the mainstay of the fleet right through to deregulation, privatisation and eventual acquisition by FirstGroup in 1997.

Most unusual features of this fleet?: The Southampton & Itchen Floating Bridge, a chain ferry from Woolston to Chapel, was acquired by the tramways department in September 1934 and was kept running until a proper bridge opened in 1977.

Anything else a bit odd?: Professor Cave-Brown-Cave – he of the radiator-cum-heating system fitted most widely in Bristol Lodekkas – developed his ideas at Southampton University and used corporation Arab IIIs as testbeds.

ALM

One of Southampton's AEC Swifts, bodied locally by Strachans of Hamble with bodies similar to London Transport's XMS class AEC Merlins.
Michael Dryhurst

T. H. BARTON
Genius or Eccentric?

ALAN OXLEY considers the amazing achievements of a famous engineer and busman

Barton (signature)

SOMEONE who was born over 130 years ago could be forgiven for not having the knowledge of modern technology. However, there was one man who was many years ahead of his time. Over a 40-year period, from the inception of motorised transport, he experimented and introduced ideas that were both zany and forward-thinking.

Born in 1866 at Duffield, Derbyshire, Thomas Henry Barton left school with the bare essentials of education, but during a three-and-a-half year apprenticeship with Ruston Hornsby Ltd of Grantham, he learned his engineering skills. He then progressed to Manchester working on torpedo boat boilers, which led to engine room work on the *Lord Walden* travelling the China Seas. Returning home via Russia, he travelled from St Petersburg over to the east coast, fixing lighting on railway stations.

Following his marriage, he gained employment with Manlove Alliott & Co, constructing, developing and repairing internal-combustion gas engines. During this period he attended Professor Robinson's classes at the Nottingham University College technical workshops. Professors Robinson and Simpson were at that time acquiring data on gas and oil engines.

In 1890, he returned to Ruston Hornsby, and was soon working almost exclusively on the Ackroyd Stuart hot bulb crude oil engine which had been patented and built on an experimental basis. However, it was far from satisfactory and under the direction of Robert Edwards, the chief engineer, he became involved in the development of the Hornsby-Ackroyd engine. The introduction of a cam-operated fuel-injection pump was a key step forward in the development of the oil engine and important improvements were made in other features. T. H. Barton never acknowledged Diesel, claiming the credit for the first successful oil engine belonged to England not Germany, as the Ackroyd Stuart engine was the forerunner of all oil engines developed.

Quarry

During 1894, he was back in Derbyshire to take over the family quarry, but not before he had been presented with an engine by Hornsbys, following his successful work with them. Unfortunately the quarry was not a flourishing business, so leaving it to a manager, he moved yet again, with his family, this time to Mablethorpe on the Lincolnshire coast. It was here that he first became involved in transporting passengers, using a pony trap to and from the station. This often occasional work was supplemented by collecting scrap iron.

Visiting a London exhibition in 1897 with son Tom and daughter Kate, he took the decision to purchase a 9hp Benz-engined 11-passenger vehicle. This had a belt-driven single-cylinder engine fitted to a small modified horse wagonette, with two speeds and no reverse. Following a very eventful three-day journey, during which time they all had plenty of opportunity to learn to drive, it was then put to work carrying passengers between the 'Pullover' and Victoria Road, Mablethorpe, and must have been one of the earliest petrol-engined buses to operate in the British Isles.

Barton and his family returned to Derbyshire in the winter, and began to operate between Little Eaton and Derby. With a change of vehicles, he then spent time in Weston-super-Mare, Duffield, Tansley near Matlock, and Derby.

Following a move to Beeston in 1908, he ran a service between Long Eaton and Nottingham, during the first week of October, to transport passengers to the famous Goose Fair, which was so popular that he was able establish a regular service between Nottingham and Beeston, with some journeys extended to Long Eaton.

T. H. Barton, as painted by Norman Hepple. This portrait was presented to 'The Guv'nor' in 1944 by his employees to mark the award of the OBE.
Alan Oxley collection

Reputation

With these early forays into bus operation he was becoming well known and certainly was gaining a reputation and was even asked to take over an established route between Llandaff Castle and Cardiff Town Hall. Afterwards he was quoted as saying, 'The vehicles were obstinate, ran irregularly and the whole concern would have done credit to a first class music hall entertainment, which was certainly too good an institution to attempt to spoil'. He was also approached by the Merthyr Tydfil local authority to provide a bus service to Aberfan. This was approved by the six local authorities concerned, but it is not known if this was operated, although it is possible that a double-decker Clarkson steam bus which he owned, may have been used.

As the family grew up they became involved in the business, which was operated in the name of Andrew Barton Brothers, Andrew being the second name of his eldest son Tom. T. H., the hard-headed businessman, had no conscience when it came to gender, as everyone was expected to turn their hand to whatever work was necessary. As early as 1909 an unsuccessful application was made for a conductor's licence for Mary Barton aged 20. However, by July 1913 eldest daughter Kate was driving and her sisters Ruth and Edith were conducting. The *Daily Mirror* on the 3 July 1913 carried an article on the girls, which was quite a sensation at the time, although women conductors would become commonplace during World War 1.

This gave T. H. more time to devote to repairs and maintenance. In the early days it was often necessary to work through the night to keep vehicles running. He was also dealing in vehicles, picking up buses on the cheap, which had either failed mechanically or financially. Very often the lack of experience or knowledge had resulted in buses coming on to the market, which Barton had running again and then sold on to other operators. There was at least one case when a car was sold on, and one of the sons was dispatched with the vehicle, staying with the purchaser until he was confident enough to drive.

One batch of 30 vehicles in various stages of assembly came from the bankrupt Rykneild Motor Co of Burton-on-Trent, some of which were sold on, including 10 to Argentina. Young Tom persuaded his father to run one of these, upon which they built a body in a week. Although very successful it was too small for the purpose and so to increase the capacity,

Above: **It was quite a sensation in 1913 when the national press discovered that T. H. Barton was employing his three daughters on the buses. On the picture taken at Ellis Grove, Beeston, are Ruth and Edith who were employed as conductors, and in the centre is Kate, the driver. In the background is Rykneild bus AL 2360. In their spare time the girls helped mother on the two stocking frames T. H. had acquired for additional income.**
Alan Oxley collection

Right: **The maximum single-deck seating capacity that could be obtained without altering the dimensions was ingeniously achieved by fixing a set of seats on top of each front wing on Rykneild AL 1700. The driver's view must have been impaired, although the passengers would have had warm feet, even though the rest of the body was exposed to the elements.**
Alan Oxley collection

two rows of seats were ingeniously fitted longitudinally alongside the bonnet, on top of the wings. A decision was made to increase the length of a chassis by cutting it in half and inserting a section of metal to extend the wheelbase. This procedure, using timber or metal sections, was repeated on other Rykneilds, and many more vehicles over a period of 40 years.

The bus side of the operation became Progress Motor Services Ltd, and the engineering division remained as Andrew Barton Bros.

On 16 April 1913, a patent was granted for the securing of a band to a wheel. The principle was to drive bolts or distance pieces into the space between the wheel and the solid rubber or other band, so as to fix concentrically with the wheel. The space between the wheel and the tyre being filled with hot sulphur or other cement. At least one of the Rykneilds was so fitted.

Gas buses

With the outbreak of World War 1, Progress had to reduce services, which now also ran between Nottingham-Sandiacre and Long Eaton-Draycott, to conserve petrol supplies. Undaunted, T. H., remembering his days working with gas engines, introduced vehicles driven by town gas. The main problem was the difficulty of carrying gas in sufficient quantity, and this was overcome by fitting a large rubberised canvas bag – with stitched seams – on the roof, with a 6in board fixed to brackets to hold it in place. The gas was taken direct from the mains by hose, and was fed from the bag to the engine. Initial starting was made with the petrol, switching over to gas once the engine was warm. This system, which was known locally as the 'Gas Bag', was patented by Barton Bros, who manufactured these in adapted greenhouses opposite their new premises at Chilwell, some 200yd from their

original Beeston yard. Many were sold to other transport operators throughout the UK, with the Barton patent number clearly shown on photographs of the period. 'Gas Bags' were even fitted to their own Model Ford T car, a tractor, and a local customer took delivery of a trailer unit to attach to his Ford car.

There are many stories related by the locals, who found the journeys slow but were appreciative of some form of transport. When the 'Gas Bags' were low the canvas sagged and often dropped below the passengers' level of vision. On windy days the buses were difficult to steer and it was not unknown for the bags to be blown off into the most awkward places. Sunday joints often took a lot longer to cook, due to the drop in gas pressure in the district when Barton was topping up the gas bags at the Chilwell garage. It is almost certain the passengers were not aware of the dangers of travelling in the vehicles, as they were lit with acetylene lamps, which were suspended from the wooden slatted ceilings upon which the gas bags rested, and yet there were never any reported cases of explosions or fire damage!

During this time he experimented with a Daimler train, which looked a good proposition for carrying

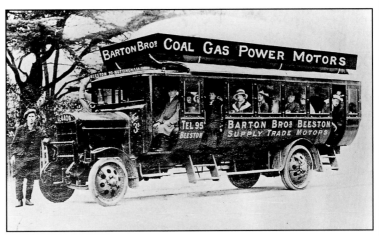

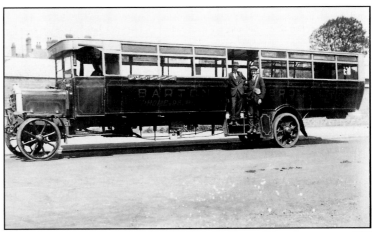

Above: **AL 4408, a Thornycroft J, had been a lorry prior to receiving this 32-seat body. Note the advertising on the boards supporting the 'Gas Bag'.**
Alan Oxley collection

Right: **'Long Tom', Daimler Y no.10, photographed opposite the company headquarters at Chilwell. It was a similar length to a present 11m coach, but by no means as comfortable.**
Alan Oxley collection

workers to the National Shell Filling Factory at Chilwell. However, the engine was difficult to start, and consumed vast amounts of petrol. Carriages were never built, although it was run with the chassis of the train. Colonel Renard, a French engineer, had designed the Renard Road Train in 1902, consisting of six-wheeled carriages each having a drive shaft and differential coupled to the drive transmitted from the rear axle of the train. Daimler obtained the British rights to manufacture these in 1907.

Stretched

The company changed its name from Progress to Barton Brothers Ltd, and during the 1920s, as manufacturers' designs and vehicles generally improved, T. H. was busying himself with more ideas. Early on, former War Department and LGOC Daimler and AEC double-deckers were obtained with 34 or 36 seats, and by extending the chassis were carrying 64 seated passengers. These were nothing compared to two further stretched Daimlers; the first, no.8, was 34ft 2in long with seating for 60 and space for a further 40 standing within the central entrance single-deck body. The second arrived a little later during January 1923 and was given fleet no.10; although identical in looks it was 36ft 6in long, with seating for 66 passengers. They were each about 10ft longer than the contemporary normal full-sized bus. It was T. H.'s idea to have a generator attached to the chassis, providing an efficient lighting system whilst the engine was running, and made a big saving on batteries which at that time had a rather short life.

Needless to say, these vehicles did not pass without incident, as again recalled by locals who had a great affection for the company, and who named them both 'Long Tom'. To give extra strength, steel bracings were

Left: *No.24, a Lancia-Barton with Strachan & Brown bodywork, on Derby Road, Nottingham. Extended in the Barton workshops and fitted with a second rear axle, the increased dimensions allowed for 39 seated passengers. Although the radiator retained the Lancia shape, it had been built at Chilwell in copper with brass tubing.*
Alan Oxley collection

Below: *This Morris one-ton chassis with Strachan & Brown 24-seat body had been extended and given a third axle, which allowed an increase on the normal chassis of up to six seats.*
Alan Oxley collection

Top: *Barton's crude oil-engined bus entered service in March 1930. It incorporated a Gardner 4L2 engine in the Lancia-Barton chassis, which carried the Irish registration number XI 6375. T. H. Barton is seated in the saloon. This was the first British oil engine to be fitted to a bus and claimed to be the first in service.*
Alan Oxley collection

Above: *VO 4296, no.132, often alleged to be a Gilford, was an all-Barton product. It entered service in August 1930 having been fitted with a Gardner 5L2, and it was probably the world's first five-cylinder oil-engined bus. Although not visible in this view, the roof panels advertised this as a 'Barton British Fuel Oil Bus'. Despite being the predecessor to thousands of Gardner five-cylinder buses, it received a Commer petrol engine in June 1932.*
Alan Oxley collection

fitted across the floor on the inside of the body, which passengers regularly stumbled over; at the hump-backed canal bridge in Long Eaton, one became balanced on the top, with its wheels suspended in mid air; the entrance to Draycott in both directions was restricted by a narrow Z-bend railway bridge, in which the bus became trapped; it is known that, with the considerable rear overhang, they often knocked cyclists over when negotiating tight bends; the bounce of the rear overhang, particularly when partly loaded, kept the conductor busy replacing seat cushions which fell

to the floor at regular intervals. They did not find favour with Nottingham Corporation which would not allow them into the city and so were relegated to Gotham and Loughborough services.

Six-wheelers

By 1923 the fleet, although reliable, was proving slow and ponderous in face of competition, which was usually in the form of the faster, smaller lightweight buses with pneumatic tyres. To compete, Barton adopted the policy of 'chasing'; it is not known if the company was the first with the idea, but it quickly caught on. The idea was to place your vehicle in front of the opposition to collect all the passengers. When it stopped, a second vehicle, which lay immediately behind, overtook the rival, to take prime place for the next stop. This form of leap-frogging continued between each terminal, in the hope of running the competition into financial ruin – or the next ditch. Faster vehicles were also required for this type of work, and so it was decided to purchase Lancia chassis. Some of these were obtained through the Italian Government or through Lancia, which had repurchased vehicles after army service. These came in various forms, sometimes as armoured cars or even, it is said, as large saloon cars. The first seven had 26 seats, which may have been extended, but the next had 32 seats on an extended chassis which was 26ft 1in long. More Lancia-Barton chassis were added, and then by the end of 1924 it was possible to introduce a 36-seat model and then 39- or 40-seaters, by fitting a trailing third axle.

These were claimed to be the first six-wheeled buses introduced into regular service in the UK, although this configuration had successfully run both on the Continent and the United States. The idea of introducing this was to increase the load capacity, without exceeding the axle loadings, and, in particular at that date, the limitations of pneumatic tyres. Improved riding comfort was a feature and again through the nickname given by the locals, became known as the famous 'Barton Gliders'. An overall length of 29-30ft was achieved on certain chassis. During this period three Chevrolets, a Ford T and a Morris were similarly converted. Bodywork was by Strachan & Brown, Challands Ross and Barton (rebuilt or completely new).

An interesting Lancia-Barton six wheeler (no.107) entered the fleet in 1928. This was a Pentaiota model purchased new from Lancia, and converted at Chilwell before the fitting of a Massey body, to which Barton fitted a heating system directly from the exhaust. At its peak in 1929 the fleet contained a total of 53 six-wheelers in service.

Forward control

A further novel way to increase the seating capacity was to convert one of the Lancia chassis to forward control and fit a separate driver's cab next to the engine. This is believed to have been the only Lancia ever so operated.

Alldays Commercial Motors of Jermyn Street, London, was obviously impressed by the 'Glider' as it was offering six-wheelers with Barton patent springing and trailing axle at the 1927 Olympia exhibition. These included rebuilt Lancias and Alldays (Barton?) chassis.

During the period of the 'Glider' conversions, T. H.

was experimenting with a front-wheel drive lowfloor bus, which had been built and fitted with a body using an advanced hooped frame chassisless construction. This will be fully described in a future edition of *Classic Bus*.

Various ideas were introduced in the workshops at Chilwell, including overhead electric wires, on to which were hooked various attachments, providing an early type of trailing lead. There was also an engine test bed, where a completed engine ran on town gas, with the radiator connected to the water supply. This was attached to a shaft with belts which then drove several engines in various stages of repair. When the slave engine was run in and removed the remainder were moved along and another part rebuilt engine added. A mobile electric starter motor (nicknamed the 'Pig') was also built, this was connected by the means of a square spigot on to the bus, thus avoiding manual winding starting handles.

In 1928 Barton applied unsuccessfully to operate a coupled coach. Regrettably there are no details, and an investigation with former workers produced nothing, but it is assumed that this was an idea that could have been produced if given sanction. We can only surmise what might have been envisaged. Whatever it was, it would have been revolutionary, and competitive with the railways, for he had scant regard for them and his forthright opinions expressed in this interview with *The Industrial World*, much of which still rings true today:

Above: **Today this would be a safety officer's nightmare, as this device provided electricity in the form of a trailing lead. Two live electric wires were suspended around the workshops providing a supply from which was hooked a lead for various attachments.**
Alan Oxley collection

"We are of the opinion that services, such as ours, are of the greatest possible advantage to the country at large. To open up new routes which it would be impossible for a railway to cover. We are prepared for every emergency, and you will appreciate that it is quite possible for a district to spring into popularity be heavily populated, and then fade away before ever a rail bill could be passed through Parliament. The motor bus is ready whenever it is wanted, to go where-ever needed. And there is no loss when the necessity for working the route disappears. But a railway — well, it is impossible to cope with such circum-stances.

The railways are gradually becoming obsolete, owing to the apathy and conceit of railway engineers, who have blinded themselves to progress, and considered their position unassailable. The loco-motive and rolling stock of today is hopelessly out of date. The top heavy, dangerous build of a locomotive, we consider, is not really safe at over 40 miles per hour, except on the straightest bit of railway.

If the rolling stock and permanent way was re-designed on modern en-gineering principles, there is no way why an express train should not make the journey from Nottingham to London, 120 miles, in the hour, and thus try to get back the business they have lost by their apathy and the false security, in which they have passed the last 20 years. Thinking their monopoly was impregnable, and they could make their own terms with the public, whom they considered were at their mercy for transport facilities."

Left: *No.348, one of a batch of four Leyland TD5s with Duple lowbridge forward entrance bodywork delivered in 1939. The high finish of coachwork specified by Barton included a clock and for the only time in double-deckers in this or any other fleet, radios were provided. Electro-pneumatically-operated sliding doors were another feature, which had been successfully used on the dual-purpose saloons.*
G. H. F. Atkins

Left: *This 'Gas Bag' trailer was originally fitted to Leyland LT8 no.350, but T. H. decided to increase the original height by 4ft and converted no.247, an AEC Regent with forward entrance Willowbrook body accordingly. The addition can be seen on this photograph taken at Parliament Street, Nottingham. However, this was short-lived, as the trailer was very unstable, particularly in high winds. The Regent dated from 1934 and came into the fleet when the Campion of Nottingham business was acquired in 1935.*
Alan Oxley collection

A further patent was granted to T. H., for the fireproofing of petrol tanks. This involved surrounding the tank with a lockable outer metal casing with air space between, making it more accessible and readily removable when damaged. The risk of fire was reduced if started from the carburettor, as it would travel along the feed pipe, but the compartment would restrict the flames access to the tank, and also if fire broke out in the tank itself it was possible by shutting the door to prevent further combustion.

Oil engines

The last Lancia-Barton chassis were produced in 1931, but even more interesting was the introduction in 1929 of the company's own chassis. The first two, nos.110 and 120, were to normal control layout with Meadows petrol engines, and bodywork by Challands Ross and Barton respectively. A further 16 (nos.128-40/4-5/7) were built over the next three years, fitted with Coventry Climax, Commer, Continental, Dorman and Sunbeam petrol engines, and Blackstone, Barton and Gardner oil engines. Some were built in halfcab form by a variety of bodybuilders, and Barton itself. Although the last chassis were built in 1932, after the Road Traffic Act had been implemented, they only survived a short period, with the last being withdrawn in November 1936.

During a visit to the Shipping and Machinery Exhibition during August 1929, the two Tom Bartons became very interested in an oil engine exhibited for the first time by L. Gardner & Sons Ltd. The 4L2 crude oil

Above: *The 'Gas Bag' was reintroduced early in World War 2 and no.336, a Leyland Lion with Duple dual-purpose body, was one of the early recipients along with T. H. Barton's Wolseley car. Note the 'Gas Bags' were now enclosed in a timber structure.*
Alan Oxley collection

engine was built for marine work, and the company was rather surprised when Barton suggested it would be adapted for a road vehicle, and raised a number of objections before it would sell. However, Barton enthusiasm overcame the objections and on 28 February 1930, 4L2 engine unit no.28423 left Patricroft for Chilwell. This was then fitted to Lancia-Barton no.78 using Thornycroft universal joints, and a Lancia gearbox and back axle. The bus entered service during March on the Nottingham-Coalville service, accompanied for several weeks by a Gardner representative who obtained data on the operational conditions. This was to be the first British oil-engined bus to enter service, although an earlier AEC had been introduced as an experimental oil bus in December 1928, and a Sheffield Corporation Karrier with a Mercedes-Benz engine began work just after Barton no.78. Altogether four Gardner engines (including a 5L2) were purchased, but were sold to C. Fitzhugh & Co of Smethwick in June 1932. A Blackstone oil engine fitted into no.139 was returned to the manufacturer at Stamford within eight months.

All the buses that had been converted carried displays on the roof or waistrail stating 'Barton British Crude (or Fuel) Oil Bus'. The first conversion ran on crude oil, which was a by-product of the new low carbonisation plant of the Nuneaton Gas Company, and it is assumed that was not a success, as it changed to standard fuel oil. Interestingly the name Diesel was not mentioned.

Separate business

When Barton Transport Ltd was formed as a quoted public company, Barton Brothers Ltd continued as a separate business, operating from a foundry in Beck Street, Nottingham, with T. H. and his son Alfred directing operations. They produced high-class iron and metal works which included radiators for the Lancia-Barton buses and its own chassis, and manhole covers. Engineering and welding was also undertaken. T. H. now had the premises to develop his ideas, firstly producing a four-cylinder oil engine of aluminium construction, achieving lightness, trouble-free lubrication and easy replacement of cylinder liners. One was fitted to Barton no.147, but was replaced within two months with an engine from a Gilford bus. Further engines were produced which were fitted into lorries and tug-type boats used for towing barges along the River Trent to the Humber. One, however, was sold to the Paisley Omnibus Co, which fitted this into a Crossley bus.

T. H.'s interest in oil engines continued with the introduction of a diesel combustion head, suitable for fitting to a petrol side-valve engine. It is known the

Above: *The Ministry of War Transport instructed 57 of the large provincial operators to convert to gas operation using producer gas trailers, and Barton received its allocation, but T. H. must have felt there was room for improvement when he produced his own version. This was made up with old silencer boxes adapted as chimneys when demonstrated on the back of the 'Gas Bag' Wolseley. T. H. is assisted by his son-in-law Sid Nudd, who later became a partner in Nudd Bros & Lockyer.*
Alan Oxley collection

head was applied to a Commer 4PF engine, upon which tests were made, but it did not run in passenger service. A single-valve oil engine was also patented, which, although not fully developed, was sold on to Packard of America, which built the engine using the Barton principles; it was fitted into an aeroplane and it is believed to be the only occasion this was so used.

He also had ideas for car parking, patenting and building a unit which housed three cars in the space of one, by providing lift cages which could be raised or lowered above or below floor level.

Various ideas were introduced in the workshops at Chilwell, including overhead electric wires, on to which were hooked various attachments, providing an early type of trailing lead. There was also an engine test bed, where a completed engine ran on town gas, with the radiator connected to the water supply. This was attached to a shaft with belts which then drove several engines in various stages of repair. When the slave engine was run in and removed the remainder were moved along and another part rebuilt engine added. A mobile electric starter motor (nicknamed the 'Pig') was also built, this was connected by the means of a square spigot on to the bus, thus avoiding manual winding starting handles.

The outbreak of World War 2 again saw the introduction of 'Gas Bags' in a more refined form. The bags were now contained within a plywood-covered framework. The first vehicle so converted, no.336, had the frame extended down the back of the

bus, giving a 5ft extension, which unfortunately did not meet the approval of the Traffic Commissioners who requested the immediate removal of the increased vehicle length. Twenty-eight single-deckers in total were converted, as were two Morris 10cwt vans and at least two Wolseley cars. No.247, an AEC Regent forward entrance double-decker, was fitted with a 'Gas Bag' trailer, which was short-lived, as the lightweight trailer was very unstable, particularly in high winds. Producer gas trailers were also introduced on Ministry of War Transport instructions, and T. H. built one of these to his own specification, using old silencer boxes for chimneys.

Honour

T. H. Barton, who became an OBE in the King's Birthday Honours list in June 1943, passed away on 26 July 1946, aged 80. Under the direction of Tom junior and his brothers, the firm continued in good

hands. The sons kept up their father's traditions and during the early 1950s once again started extending chassis in various forms until 1971. For a period after the war, coachbuilding was re-established. The Bartons also had their own ideas, including the fitting of oil replenishers on many of the buses, which reduced the evening oil checks to a weekly operation. Following the Chatham disaster, when several sea cadets were hit and killed by a bus whilst marching in badly-lit streets, Barton decided to develop a safety device on its own vehicles. This was a patented lighting switch which operated when the sidelamps were switched on, and automatically illuminated the dipped nearside lamp as soon as the vehicle moved, or extinguished it when it came to rest.

I remember very vividly, as a nine-year old, being at Chilwell garage to see the funeral cortege leaving with the coffin of T. H. placed on a Leyland chassis. That was my only meeting with him, but I already had an interest which had been sparked by the stories told by my relatives. Over many years I have recorded and researched the company and T. H. Barton, the man known as 'The Guv'nor', 'The Old Man' – I even heard him called 'Captain Kettle', no doubt from the fact he always wore a peaked cap and a half-knotted tie. Although of diminutive stature he was a real powerhouse both in work and in the little leisure time he had.

Above: **The Government approved the increase in maximum dimensions for passenger vehicles during 1950, which allowed the length of a single decker to be increased from 27ft 6in x 7ft 6in to 30ft x 8ft. After a lapse of 20 years the workshops were again using their skills, influenced by T. A. Barton and his brothers, who had so much experience in this work. By purchasing some of the many prewar Leyland Titans now on the market it was possible to cut a 15ft front and rear section from two 26ft long chassis and weld them together. The first four were bodied at Beccols and Strachans, but the fifth received a Barton body. Only five received this style of 'Viewmaster' body, although more were built in a further two distinctive designs. No.634 was photographed outside the Chilwell headquarters, with T. A. and Maurie Barton in attendance. The design was unusual, as they had tried to achieve the maximum visibility for the driver. The chassis was now classified as a Barton BTS/I, being made up of two Burnley Leyland Titan TD3cs, nos.93 and 98.**
Alan Oxley collection

I have come to the conclusion that the industry did not take him seriously. Was it because he worked out in the sticks, lacked the capital and resources – or just that he was ahead of his time? At least I have now had the opportunity to state his case and hope that he will be included as one of the passenger transport greats of the 20th century. **CB**

THE AEC Reliance was one of the two great British underfloor-engined single-deckers of the 1950s, 1960s and 1970s and, indeed, also was one of a handful of models – the Leyland Atlantean and Bedford SB are probably the only others – to have survived in production for more than 25 years. And it was the last psv chassis to carry the legendary AEC name.

Three good reasons, I argue, why it qualifies for Wonderbus status. A fourth, and here we're getting into the usual subjective stuff in which most of us enthusiasts indulge, is that for most of its production life it sounded special. Lots of AEC whines – whether it came with the more common manual gearbox or the different distinctive melodies of the Monocontrol semi-automatic – plenty of throaty exhaust notes and some delightful wheezes from somewhere deep down in the drivetrain or braking system.

It also deserves an accolade for the way it evolved with the changing demands of the operating industry from its launch in 1953 until 1979, when it was finally killed off in the first seismic shifts of the catastrophic earthquake that was to destroy much of British Leyland.

For the Reliance first hit the market as a medium-weight chassis, a sort of Dennis Dart of its day, answering an urgent – if, truth be told, misguided – demand for lighter-weight, economical models to take the place of the battleship-like first generation underfloor-engined single-deckers like AEC's Regal IV and Leyland's Royal Tiger.

CLASSIC
WONDER
BUS

In every issue of *Classic Bus* magazine, ALAN MILLAR nominates a Classic Blunderbus, looking at models that never quite made it. In the Yearbook, he offers you the AEC Reliance as a Classic *Wonder*bus

It ended its life as a totally different beast, a large-engined heavy duty coach more in the mould of Volvo's B10M. Before it was axed without a universally

Below: *The Reliance was originally conceived by AEC as a medium-weight chassis, and found favour in bus form with BET group companies like Yorkshire Woollen. This is a 1959 2MU3RV model with 43-seat BET-style Park Royal body.*

Left: When 36ft long buses and coaches were permitted in 1961, a longer Reliance was introduced. An early customer for this was OK of Bishop Auckland, with this 1962 Plaxton Highway-bodied example.

Leyland answered that demand in 1959 with the Leopard which, when launched, was effectively a Tiger Cub with a bigger engine and which later grew into 11 and 12m chassis; the Tiger Cub steadily faded out of the picture.

AEC's answer was to keep the Reliance name, but to transform the product. In 1957, the export version was made bigger and stronger and given the curious internal designation of 'heavy medium-weight'; then in 1960, when most operators appeared to favour the 7.7-litre AH470 engine option over the 6.7-litre AH410, an unashamedly heavy duty Reliance was introduced with the 9.6-litre AH590, and a 36ft version followed in 1961 with beefier chassis frame and axles. Had Leyland kept the Tiger Cub name or had AEC called its heavy duty model something else like Renown, then the Reliance might not have been seen as the long-lived Wonderbus that it was.

Today, we also look upon it as part of a cohesive AEC family of buses, in the tradition that also brought us the Regent, Regal and Routemaster, but in 1953 it represented a radical departure from the company's existing product range – far more so, in fact, than happened when the Regal IV had been launched only four years earlier. As Alan Townsin wrote in his *Blue Triangle* book on AEC, this was the first time since 1929 that an AEC had been produced with an entirely new chassis and key components; only the horizontal AH410 had been seen before, and that was in vertical form as the Regal II's A172.

It was a sound move, for the Reliance broadened AEC's customer base. Consider the likes of East Kent, North Western and Aldershot & District, all BET subsidiaries which had tended to buy elsewhere before. The East Kent and A&D orders were interesting, too, for their Reliances succeeded in killing off Dennis's ambitions of becoming a major player in the mid-engined single-deck market; and the Reliance did AEC a further favour by persuading East Kent to switch from the Guy Arab to its new single-decker supplier's Regent V for double-deck deliveries.

There was a lot more, too, for many other BET fleets – notably PMT, Devon General, Northern General, Maidstone & District and South Wales bought substantial numbers, while the Scottish Bus Group departed from an earlier huge pro-Leyland bias to take over 600 Reliances from the mid-1950s to the mid-1960s – nearer 800 if you throw in the short-lived

acceptable replacement, it was the coach chassis that many operators aspired to own and significant numbers chose to buy.

Enormous success

And it's worth saluting the fact that the Reliance was one AEC which enjoyed enormous success – sales well in excess of 8,000 vehicles during its long production run – without more than the token support of London Transport. Many other British chassis sold well without the benefit of cheques posted out of 55 Broadway, SW1, but AEC was different. It had grown out of the chassis-building department of the old London General Omnibus Company in 1912 and, although the formal ties had long since been severed, there still was an impression that the two organisations were joined at the hip and that many AEC products were designed with at least half an eye on the needs of its biggest bus client.

Partly because it had just invested in 700 RF-class Regal IVs, LT had little need for more single-deckers; it bought only 17 Reliances for its own fleet and eight more for British European Airways. This was a chassis for the rest of the market, and one which sold widely and in consistently healthy numbers for many years.

It's only fair to say that, yes, the Reliance also had its weaknesses, not least a propensity to overheat in intensive service, but boiling buses were more common in the past than, happily, they are today and the Reliance was not alone in working itself up into a lather.

Longevity

And it's also fair to say that AEC cheated a little with the longevity. Or was it Leyland that cheated? Let me explain. The Reliance was AEC's solution to a challenge which Leyland had answered a year earlier with its broadly similar Tiger Cub. Within a few years, as 36ft (11m) chassis were in the offing and some of the weaknesses of lightweight components and small engines were beginning to manifest themselves, operators began looking for more powerful, heavier duty chassis.

Left: **London Country dubbed its Duple Dominant II-bodied Reliances RB (Reliance Blackpool). RB16, seen when new, was among the first of 150 Reliance 6U2Rs (154bhp AH691 engines) bought in 1977-9 to update the Green Line fleet. The 150 Reliances included 60 RSs (Reliance Scarborough, bodied by Plaxton).**

batch of left-hand-drive models for a short-lived international service to Athens. And of course there was the London connection.

Influential

LT may only have bought 17 Reliances, but they were influential. The first three, the RW class of 1960, were short two-door experimental one-person operated buses for the old country area; they lasted just three years before being sold to Chesterfield Corporation. But 1965 saw the 14 RC-class Green Line coaches arrive, another experimental batch which suffered from being oddities in a huge fleet of RFs, but which clearly pleased the right people a few years later.

For the Reliance became synonymous with the last years of Green Line as we knew it. London Country, the new NBC company formed to take over the country area in 1970, bought 90 with Park Royal bodies and although it was later obliged to take less-than-inspiring Leyland Nationals for these long-distance services, a change of heart in 1977 saw a move to leasing 'proper' coaches and the favoured chassis – at a time when most NBC fleets took Leopards – was the Reliance. Eventually, 150 were run and there would have been more had fate not intervened.

By then, Leyland was rationalising and trying to make the world believe the Reliance had become a Leyland-badged product, even though most went on the road with the proper blue triangular logos with the first, fifth and third letters of the alphabet. It wanted to replace the Leopard and Reliance with a new chassis which would emerge in 1981 as the Tiger, but other pressures were bearing down harder and the axe fell on the under-employed AEC factory at Southall in 1979. With it died the Reliance.

Independent-minded

Its coach operator fans didn't want that to happen and nor, it seems, did at least some clued-up people within Leyland Bus who saw, correctly, that many of those independent-minded buyers would rather purchase imported products than a Leyland they had chosen not to buy before; not even the addition of the Reliance's ZF gearbox was enough to make some of them take the Leopard. Many deserted Leyland forever.

So even in death, the Reliance was such a Wonderbus that it cast a shadow over its biggest British-built rival. Evidence indeed that AEC's last PSV was a force to respect. **CB**

Monocoach cousin which shared its major running unit specification with early Reliances.

Oddities

Municipals bought them, too, albeit seldom building up collections of more than 20 in days when most favoured double-deckers, but those and notable independent purchases included some unusual vehicles; the municipal oddities included five with central entrances for Leeds, six short Pennine-bodied models for Great Yarmouth and 10 wide-entrance Alexander Y-types for Dundee, while few independent purchases were much odder than six Yeates Europas for Barton. Apart from Barton, larger independent customers for the Reliance included Lancashire United, Premier Travel and Yelloway.

By the mid-1960s, the Reliance faced new threats to its future. The 1962 Leyland/AEC 'merger' helped persuade SBG and many of the former BET companies absorbed into the National Bus Company to buy Leopards and other Leyland products instead; and the move towards rear-engined chassis turned some bus customers on to AEC's new Swift – a model that, sadly, is unlikely ever to grace these particular pages in a *Classic Bus Yearbook*. But the faithful old chassis kept adapting itself.

Since the late-1950s, AEC had been offering an option of air suspension and had gone on to work with PMT on a version with rubber suspension. German-made ZF gearboxes came in during the early 1960s and the engine options kept getting bigger. The 8.1-litre AH505 replaced the AH470 in 1964 and the 11.3-litre AH691 replaced the AH590 in 1966. In 1972, the 12.5-litre AH760 – later redesignated L12 when it became a Leyland truck engine – replaced the 691, and the 505 was dropped two years later.

By then, much of its surviving business was with independent coach operators, but NBC bought a small

HEAVER

MARTYN NUTLAND traces the history of a West Country coachbuilder

Left: *Heaver was a consistent supplier to Guernsey. The smart and workmanlike treatment of a Leyland Cub (circa 1930) is from one of the earlier orders and flourishes the popular Heaver feature of valancing from screen pillar base to front wing.*

ASK ANY bus and coach enthusiast to name a handful of bodybuilders and you could virtually guarantee firms like Duple, Park Royal, Willowbrook and Plaxton would be listed. Delve for the slightly more obscure and marques like Mann Egerton, Burlingham and Saunders might come up. Yet few are likely to cite the name of Heaver Limited although this West Country firm traded for more than 40 years, at its peak employed upwards of 40 craftsmen and built for dozens of companies in regions hundreds of miles from its Wiltshire home.

John Thomas Heaver was a Londoner by birth and lived in Shepherd's Bush in the days when trees lined nearby Chiswick High Street, horse buses and trams rattled through the city's cobbled streets and the Salvation Army marched around the Green on a Sunday morning with little but the occasional passage of the latter to draw them earthwards.

Mr Heaver worked as a trimmer for a highly acclaimed carriage-maker called Peters and at the outbreak of World War 1 was already a married man with a small son. By 1915 he had been drafted into the Army and posted to Bulford Camp in Wiltshire as a member of the Army Service Corps. The military establishment still sprawls along the edge of Salisbury plain engulfing the villages of Bulford and Durrington.

Mr Heaver's role was to finish and repair some of the thousands of motorised vehicles being pressed into service in the first predominantly mechanised war in history. And such was the demand for his and his compatriots' skill in making and refurbishing hoods, canopies and tilt covers that Mr Heaver remained at Bulford for the duration.

Coach trade

When he was eventually demobilised John Heaver decided he would settle in Durrington and set up business in the coach trade. To this end a former builder's yard in the village's main street, with ample room for expansion, was acquired. Mr Heaver was soon joined by a friend from Army days called Baggett. The very first commission they received, fortuitously, in that it established the direction of the business early on, was for a charabanc-style body on an AEC chassis.

Above: **This early postwar Commer Commando for Blue Bird, Guernsey, is evocatively posed outside the St Peter Port agent for the make. It has unusual step-waist coachwork, given the seats appear to be on one level, while the streamlined sidelights, bumper and chromed radiator shell and front nave plates, are attractive touches.**

The client was an operator in Manchester called Catterall. Why business should come from so far afield in the life of the new company remains something of a mystery.

Remember, circa 1912/13 the War Office had initiated a subsidy scheme for lorries of an approved specification. Classed as 'heavy' tenders, their approved payload was actually only three tons, although in reality they frequently carried double. The idea was that civilian firms could buy these certificated vehicles with a £50 government purchase grant supplemented by a £20 annual subsidy over three years towards running and maintenance. The downside was that the authorities could reclaim the vehicles at their current value, plus 25 per cent, in times of emergency and the owner had to deliver his prized possession within 72 hours!

On the manufacturers' side the main benefactors of the scheme were Crossley, Leyland and, of course, the Associated Equipment Company – already makers of London's buses, although it was some time before that phrase was to be adopted as an AEC slogan. No fewer than 10,000 'subsidy' three-ton AECs – by far the biggest individual contribution – went to war and many survived, were recovered, and reconditioned to be sold on in 1918/19. As such they formed the backbone, not only of many postwar haulage fleets, but also of passenger undertakings.

Was this the Catterall scenario? Was he another Army friend from Bulford camp and the AEC a familiar Army surplus three-tonner he acquired with a view to exploiting the booming postwar leisure industry and its insatiable desire for mobility? What we do know is that the completed AEC impressed all and sundry, because shortly afterwards Heaver Ltd had the good fortune to secure a contract from Ford dealer, Pass & Co of Newbury, to build a landaulet version of the Model T.

Henry Ford is reputed to have said that 'Flivver' customers could have any colour they wished, as long as it was black. The same dictate was more or less true of coachwork, the vast majority of 'black' Fords being five-seat tourers.

Landaulet

The availability of a quality landaulet (a design which features a folding canopy over the rear seats with conventional coachwork to the rest of the car) would have enabled Pass, on the one hand, to extend its customer base to a more affluent clientele. But, probably more importantly, have given it the opportunity to penetrate the hackney carriage market where landaulet bodywork was popular.

Readers old enough to remember Bertram Mills Circus may also recall their Krazy taxi as one of the keynote acts and employing a Model T Ford landaulet, although I do not claim that this was of Heaver manufacture! John Heaver, son of John Thomas, recalls that there was nothing lighthearted about the construction of the Pass & Co vehicles.

The bare chassis were driven from Newbury to Durrington, the bodies built over several weeks and then the coachwork thoroughly tested for rattles and leaks before the completed vehicle was returned for sale in the company's Berkshire catchment area.

As Heaver Ltd's reputation spread, orders flowed from further and further afield. One of the most interesting, and indeed challenging, builds the company undertook in the 1920s was for the Falla family of Guernsey. In fact, the association, was so successful that the two families became personal friends.

Guernsey regulations

Guernsey carriage regulations required a bus's width to be 1ft less than on the United Kingdom mainland and the only readily available chassis that fitted the requirements at the time of Falla's order was the American Reo whose British representative was at Beaver Lane, in Hammersmith, London. Reo was the commercial vehicle arm of the American Oldsmobile auto company founded, in 1901, by R. E. Olds – hence both names.

Above: **Words add little to this study of Heaver's interpretation of the classic British halfcab coach of the late prewar and immediate postwar years, built here on a Crossley SD42.**

In 1924 it launched a vehicle called, poetically, the Speedwagon on the British market. It was designed to win business from the many small operators of which our earlier friend, Catterall, would have been one, and Falla another. The Speedwagon was powered by a four-cylinder 27hp petrol engine and, significantly, a three-speed gearbox. It remained in production until 1928 when it was replaced by the Pullman model which had a six-cylinder engine of the same output and a similar three-speed transmission.

Also on offer to British operators was a model described as the Golden Crown which had the same engine but a four-speed 'box and hydraulically, as opposed to mechanically, operated brakes. The latter ceased production in 1931 while the Pullman lasted until 1933. Unfortunately, Heaver never kept a record of the bodies they built so there is no definitive evidence of what was what and what went where.

However, it seems likely that Falla's bus was built on a six-cylinder Pullman chassis, because we know from John Heaver's recollections that the body gave total satisfaction, but performance over island roads proved the vehicle to be unsuitably geared. This suggests the three-speed gearbox and fairly 'effete' six-cylinder motor, as opposed to the 'torquey' four-cylinder 'slogger' of the Speedwagon.

In the end it was a good old British – or more precisely, Scottish – company that came to the rescue,

Below: **Beautifully proportioned by Heaver in 1947, is this 1935 Leyland TS7T belonging to City Coach Company of Brentwood. City, one of whose directors was a former Leyland man, was a staunch advocate of the six-wheeler. Heaver rebodied 24 of City's 43-seat TS7Ts and TS7Ds, built by either Duple or Beadle, to this 39-seat centre-entrance format.**

Above: *Certainly not one of the company's most elegant styles, this approach for Greatrex of Stafford looked even more ungainly from the front! Unusually, the chassis is a Foden PVSC6.*

in the form of Albion Motors Ltd of Scotstoun, Glasgow. Again we are somewhat hampered by the lack of documentary evidence, but thanks to Mr Heaver's excellent memory and photographs of the vehicle being swung aboard a cargo ship in Weymouth harbour, we discover the Albion bought by Falla to replace their Reo was a four-cylinder Victor. One of its most salient features for the Guernsey operator would have been that Albion was prepared to build the vehicle to the required width. Mr Heaver recalls that this was achieved by leaving the chassis frame intact but fitting narrow wheels and shortened axles.

He also remembers with some discomfort one of the Victor's less appealing features. 'They had no self starter as standard equipment and I broke a small bone in my wrist as a consequence of a venomous backfire while I was trying to start the beast on the handle,' he reflects.

Falla was to remain loyal to Albion for many years the Portsmouth firm of Reading eventually holding the coachbuilding contract.

Popularity

As the 1930s progressed the list of operators that favoured Heaver grew considerably as did the tally of chassis. Not surprisingly, in view of their popularity with operators, AEC chassis were a frequent sight at Durrington. Mr Heaver recalls taking the train from the West Country to Southall, West London, armed with flying jacket and helmet, goggles and the all-important pneumatic car seat cushion, to collect the bare chassis and drive them back.

But by far the company's favourite vehicle builder was Daimler. 'They were very good to us,' remembers Mr Heaver. 'I was particularly involved with the CVD6 which succeeded the CW model in 1946 and in fact lasted, in double-deck form, beyond the end of Heaver Ltd. Lots of our customers liked this model which had an oil engine of over eight litres and the famous fluid flywheel and Wilson four-speed preselector gearbox. But above all we always had a good relationship with the sales people at Coventry.

'Going back prewar I can remember setting off from Durrington for South Wales with a coach in the early hours of the morning in the company of a Daimler salesman. We spent a whole day "over the wate", returning late in the evening, having demonstrated the vehicle to various local operators. In fact, there were some "takers" in Wales for our version.'

Personal recommendation

However, not all were success stories. Mr Heaver explains: 'Most of our business came by personal recommendation, although we did advertise in the specialist press. But one year my father decided to take a stand at the Motor Show at Olympia. We had two Daimlers, probably from the 1934-40 CO series, plus a demonstrator, but virtually no one visited our stand and we certainly took no orders, the "in-crowd" being content to hang round the big-name exhibits. Father decided, "never again!"'

There were also the coaches that Heaver itself decided were unsatisfactory. One such was the product of Foden, who achieved prowess in virtually all sectors of commercial vehicle manufacture bar that of the public service vehicle. In the late 1940s the Cheshire

Above: *Heaver bodied a number of Dennis chassis, but this is a particularly attractive treatment, thought to be for Harveys of Cheddington, Gloucestershire, on a circa 1950 Lancet J10.*

manufacturer developed a two-stroke diesel for a rear-engined single-deck bus chassis announced in 1950 as the PVR model. There was an engine option of a conventional Gardner 6LW, but the Foden unit, fitted to vehicles classified PVRF and available in four- and six-cylinder versions, had piston-controlled inlet ports and overhead poppet exhaust valves. It boasted a power-to-weight ratio of 8.5lb per brake horsepower compared to between 12lb and 15lb for the average four-stroke.

Mr Heaver remembers it as unacceptably noisy. 'It was strange. We bodied a number of Commer Avengers which used another diesel two-stroke, this time the horizontally-opposed TS3 with three cylinders and two pistons in each bore, and although they had a very distinctive sound, noise wasn't a problem. However, the Foden was very obtrusive, particularly if there was something around for the sound to resonate from, like a wall. Also, I don't think matters were helped by the coachwork which had a very flat front and created additional wind noise,' he says.

In fairness, the Foden was just ahead of its time. The two-stroke engine was successful in the company's lighter lorries and the PVR earned for the Sandbach manufacturer the distinction of being, apart from self-build operator Midland Red, first with a full-frontal facility on a standard chassis.

Continues Mr Heaver: 'It was around this time – the early 1950s – Daimler introduced the Freeline chassis with a horizontally-mounted engine, but we found it a bit high and passenger access was not ideal.' Nor was the Freeline popular with UK operators and most went overseas.

Loyal user

Although there were no exclusively 'Heaver' fleets,

Burfitt, trading as Blue Coaches of Ilfracombe, was a loyal user and Bakers of Weston-super-Mare, Burwell & District, Cooks Coaches of Westcliff-on-Sea, Harveys of Cheddington in Gloucestershire, Kings of Bath, Monarch and Silver City from Bristol, Silver Star local to Salisbury and Webbs Motor Services of Dorchester all had their quota. Further afield devotees were, of course, Falla, but also Blue Coach Tours of Jersey, City Coaches in Brentwood, Parsons at Loughton in Essex and Johnsons Supreme from Stourbridge.

Not all Heaver's work was straightforward coachbuilding. Bristol Tramways sent its Eastern Coach Works (Lowestoft)-bodied vehicles for rebuilds and reconditioning, rather than opting for the less convenient and cost-effective option of despatching them across the country to their point of origin in Lowestoft. And some work did not involve buses or coaches at all. The association with Pass & Co remained and, when the Ford Eight and Ten appeared in the mid-1930s, a stylish tourer was created at Durrington.

At the opposite end of the motoring scale was a unique project for a local doctor named Lewis. He commissioned Heaver to rebody a Bentley on the Weymann principle. Weymann was a French company which overcame the self-destructive flexing of early wooden-framed car bodies with a patented design. It insulated the coachwork from the chassis, used metal plates to avoid directly jointed timbers, then covered the whole with fabric. The process was licensed and

many attractive versions resulted. Nothing is now known about the Bentley in question, but it was probably a vintage chassis (pre-1930) whose body had deteriorated in the way described, or simply was not to the doctor's taste. Rebodying of this kind was not uncommon in the 1930s and a number of firms were engaged in the activity as a commercial enterprise.

Returning to more mundane transport, Heaver also built a fleet of AEC meat vans for a Salisbury company, constructing the basic body prior to sending them to a specialist who fitted the refrigeration plant.

Even such prosaic contracts ceased in 1939 when World War 2 began. Heaver Ltd were 'called to arms' by the Ministry of Supply and spent the period repairing a wide variety of military vehicles based in the Bulford area and particularly, at Tidworth Camp.

Served time

Few people can now know more about commercial vehicle body building as it was practised from the 1920s to the 1950s than Mr Heaver. He joined his father in the business virtually as soon as he had left school and served time in the bodyshop itself, with the panel beaters and in the forge. 'The only craft I didn't study was coach-painting,' admits Mr Heaver. 'Somehow it didn't appeal to me. The designs for the bodies were done by my father. He used a fairly informal technique working at a drawing board but not following through with full-scale patterns to which the sections would be fabricated. Once he was pleased with a shape final adjustments would be made by the foreman as the job progressed.

'Of course, there was a certain amount of "cribbing"

within the industry. For example, our bodies for the Bedford OB were very similar to the Duple Vista style which predominated on that chassis, apart from around the rear quarter. Normally, it was accepted that the mainstream styles were adapted by smaller builders, but I remember we did get into trouble once. I think it was the Foden body, or possibly some Leyland Royal Tigers we did for Johnsons that someone – Burlingham, it may have been – found rather too close to their Seagull and complained; not to us, but to the operator!'

In Heaver's heyday four bodies would be under construction simultaneously with a team of four or five men working on each one and all helping to complete the procedures in sequence. 'The first job', explains Mr Heaver, 'was to get the "deck" fixed to a chassis. You weren't allowed by the manufacturer to drill the frame so a system of clamps was used which had the advantage of making the body easily demountable for repair or exchange between vehicles. We then fitted the upright side members and nailed the aluminium body and roof panels to this basic frame.

'From there the team progressed to upholstery [Mr Heaver's late brother, George, and his nephew, Peter, were upholsterers with the company] and the general furnishing of the body.

'The wood used was seasoned American ash which was imported through Liverpool and came to Bulford by train from where it was delivered by horse and cart. We then treated it with preservative and used a

Above: **Towards the end of production at Heaver, coach design had gravitated towards a number of highly popular styles from the drawing boards of firms like Burlingham, Duple and Plaxton. Their influence is present in the mid-1950s coachwork on a still unregistered Daimler Freeline, whose similarity to a Burlingham Seagull prompted complaints!**

bandsaw powered by a Lister petrol/paraffin engine to cut the sections. The paints were bought from Culverhouse & Sons in Borough High Street, south London, who employed a salesman of the old school – moustachioed, always immaculately dressed and wearing spats!

'We never built vehicles speculatively, all our work was to order. Once we began a job there was seldom any input from the customer. However, I remember one gentleman whose main occupation was that of opera singer, but who had an Exeter coach business as a sideline. He called every Sunday morning to view progress on a body we were building for him on a Minerva chassis.

'In the case of coaches like AECs and Leylands we used to have to take them back to the works for inspection. You'd be waiting around for two or three hours while they took them away and checked you'd not done anything silly like cut through the chassis. Daimler, however, did not require anything like that from us.

Around the clock

'My father was totally committed to delivering jobs on time and, if necessary you would work around the clock to achieve that. I remember one such job which had its lighter moment. The team were battling against time to finish a body and had moved on to the next task in the sequence when, in the middle of the night, a phantom buzzer was heard aboard the coach. Investigation revealed that one of their number had been so tired he'd dropped off to sleep and slumped against the 'bell' push!'

Another story which raises a smile from John Heaver more than 40 years on, but could have had serious consequences, concerns the introduction of fibreglass front and read domes. 'We built a mould in the bodyshop to apply the compound to fibreglass matting, but within a very short time everyone was practically passing out from the fumes. We quickly sent for the supplier's representative who emphatically explained to us that the process was only intended to be undertaken in the open air or an elaborately ventilated workspace!' Those plastic sections probably wouldn't have caught on with traditionalists like Heaver Ltd anyway.

The end came in 1958. 'Following the emergence of the BET and Tilling Group companies,' explains Mr Heaver, 'bus and coach bodybuilding went to just a few large firms and there was nothing left for the dozens of little companies. We considered going into the manufacture of plastic components but without any definite plans. In the end the works was taken over by a company making motorcycle fairings.'

John Thomas Heaver died in the early 1960s, the factory which eventually grew to stand on both sides of the main road through picturesque Durrington is now a housing estate and John Heaver junior developed a new career selling Rootes commercial vehicles. **CB**